Walking Healed Companion Study

Finding Healing, Forgiveness, Grace, Hope, and Your Purpose

Mismatched Socks Productions

Walking Healed Companion Study

Copyright © 2016 Shelley Wilburn
First edition July 1, 2016
Cover photo by Deborah A. Turner
Cover model Rhiannon Wilburn
Cover by Rodney Schroeter, www.silentreels.com
Photographs by Deborah A. Turner
Edited and designed by Lisa J Lickel

All rights reserved. No part of this publication may be reproduced, stored in a retrieval system, or transmitted in any form or by any means, electronic, mechanical, photocopying, recording, or otherwise without the prior written permission of the author. Reviewers may quote briefly for review purposes.

Scripture quotations are taken from the Holy Bible, New International Version®. NIV®. Copyright © 1973, 1978, 1984 by International Bible Society. Used by permission of Zondervan. All rights reserved.

Scripture quotations are taken from the Holy Bible, New Living Translation (NLT), copyright ©1996. Used by permission of Tyndale House Publishers, Inc. Carol Stream, IL USA. All rights reserved.

Scripture quotations marked "NKJV" are taken from the New King James version. Copyright ©1982. Used by Thomas Nelson Inc. Used by permission. All rights reserved.

Scripture quotations marked HCSB are taken from the Holman Christian Standard Bible®, Copyright © 1999, 2000, 2002, 2003, 2009 by Holman Bible Publishers. Used by permission. Holman Christian Standard Bible®, Holman CSB®, and HCSB® are federally registered trademarks of Holman Bible Publishers.

Scripture quotations are taken from the Amplified Bible, Old Testament. Copyright © 1965 1987 by the Zondervan Corporation. Used by permission. All rights reserved.

Scripture quotations are taken from the Amplified Bible, New Testament. Copyright © 1954, 1958, 1987 by the Lockman Foundation. Used by permission.

Mismatched Socks Productions
ISBN 978-0-9864311-2-8
Published in the United States of America

Table of Contents

Acknowledgements iv

Introduction v

Section One: Healing Part One – Spiritual 3

    Breaking the Chains (pg. 14) 7

    God Can Still Use You (pg. 32) 8

    Take Off Your Mask (pg. 49) 9

    Shields Up! (pg. 60) 10

    Healing Rain (pg. 65) 11

    Freedom (pg. 68) 13

    Make Up Your Mind (pg. 71) 14

    Got Junk in Your Trunk? (pg. 109) 15

    Short Circuited (pg. 135) 16

    Stop People Pleasing (pg. 161) 17

    Healing: Part Two - Physical 19

Section Two: Forgiveness 29

    Part One – Forgiveness for Others 29

    Forgiveness for Others 30

    Mending Fences (pg. 17) 33

    Offense and Defense (pg. 21) 35

    Get Rid of Your "BUT!" (pg. 29) 37

    Past is Past (pg. 46) 39

    Setting Boundaries (pg. 57) 39

    Wisdom in Reconciling (pg. 77) 40

    When Friendships Fail (pg. 80) 42

    Learning to Let Go (pg. 93) 44

    Zombies…the Walking Wounded (pg. 177) 45

    Unlocking Your Door (pg. 188) 47

    Forgiveness: Part Two – Forgiveness for Yourself 49

    Do Yourself a Favor (pg. 106) 49

Section Three: Grace - Extending Grace and Receiving Grace 53

  Extending Grace (Giving Grace to Others) 54

  Moving Forward (pg. 74) 54

  Grace Who? (pg. 104) 56

  Comfort Training (111) 57

  My Chains Are Gone! (pg. 137) 60

  Because I Love You (pg. 164) 62

  Don't Back Up (pg. 168) 63

  What Are You Doing Here? (pg. 181) 66

  Where Do I Go From Here? (pg. 209) 68

Section Four: Hope 73

  Perfectly, Powerfully, and Permanently (pg. 120) 75

  Moving On! (pg. 128) 76

  Can't Keep Me Down (pg. 131) 77

  Where Do I Fit In? (pg. 133) 78

  Ch-Ch-Ch-Changes (pg. 145) 79

  I Am a Lazarus (pg. 155) 82

  Rose-Colored Glasses (pg. 174) 83

  God's Favor…is NOW! (pg. 191) 84

  Far Out! (pg. 194) 85

  Discovering My More (pg. 200) 86

  Changing Your Life (pg. 205) 87

  One More Thing 89

Section Five: Finding Your Purpose 93

  Beauty for Ashes (pg. 83) 94

  Water on the Rocks (pg. 87) 95

  Overcoming Fear (pg. 89) 97

  No One Like You (pg. 95) 98

  Don't Miss the Point (pg. 99) 99

  Answer the Phone (pg. 140) 100

  Leave Your Light On (pg. 148) 101

  Reckless (pg. 184) 103

    Snakes in the Garden (pg. 203) 105
Before We Say Good-bye 108
Appendix A: How to Memorize Scripture 109
Walking Healed Memory Verses 111
Endnotes 113
The Mismatched Socks Theory 116
About the Author 118
A Word About *Walking Healed*, the Book 119

For My Husband

Thank you for giving me the house on Saturday mornings. You sacrificed your day off and found a place to go and something to do so that this Bible study could happen. God gave me a treasure in you. Grandma Ann was right. I have such a good husband.

To My Round Table Group

When I began this journey, it never occurred to me that I would be writing a Bible study to go with Walking Healed. It also never occurred to me that opening up my home would result in the blessing of a group of women who would not only challenge me, but learn right along with me. You have been more to me than I could ever imagine. God has truly blessed me with a plethora of godly women to walk this journey with me. We have laughed, cried, prayed, and seen miracles along the way and I wouldn't have it any other way. Thank you for your time, your input, your encouragement, but mostly for your love and friendship. Ours is a bond that was forged in the realms of Heaven and will not quickly be broken. I'm sure you never imagined you would be the test run for a Bible study that was written week by week, but you came through with flying colors. You will forever own a piece of my heart and will always be my Round Table Girls; Brenda, Lanna, Kerri, Sharon, and Brynn. Our lives are forever changed, and I love you all so much.

INTRODUCTION

Walking Healed is a journey. Life is a journey. None of us have done it before. We choose to walk in healing, forgiveness, grace, hope, and our purpose daily. Therefore, we're all just muddling through life trying to figure out how to get through it with as few bumps and bruises as possible. But it doesn't always happen that way, does it? Sometimes we find ourselves smack in the middle of a crisis and wonder how we got here.

We all have struggles and trials we go through. Some may seem worse than others.

Some people seem to go through trials without an issue while others can't seem to find their way out. Nevertheless, everyone has an issue or several issues to deal with on a daily basis. Whether you struggle with depression, addiction, oppression, anxiety, illness or disease, or abuse, none is bigger or less important than another. What does matter is that you have a God who loves you dearly and never meant for you to carry this alone.

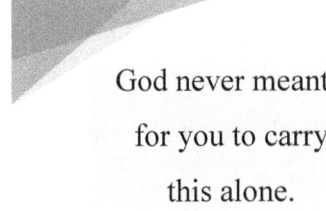

God never meant for you to carry this alone.

You may be wondering; if God loves me, why am I suffering?

It is my opinion and experience that we suffer because of sin in the world and because we have a very real enemy who hates us so he does everything he can to steal from us, kill the joy and happiness in and around us, and destroy the abundant life that God wants us to have and enjoy. As long as you stay focused on your troubles, you won't be focused on God and what His Word says about you, your life, or the lives of your children and your children's children.

But there is a way out. God helped me find it and He has asked me to help you find it, too.

Through the pages of God's Word and my book, *Walking Healed*, I am going to take you on a journey to find healing, forgiveness, grace, hope, and your purpose.

Over the next five weeks, we are going to look at each topic and read what God's Word says. By the end of the study you will hopefully be well on your way in your new journey and walking healed. You will also be equipped to help others find their new journey.

Though we journey together, each of us is on our own adventure. Trust me when I say that walking healed is a grand adventure. I would say "buckle up" but you don't want to be tied down for this journey, dear lovelies. You want to be free to move around, because during the course of this study we will be doing a lot of moving.

This study is broken up into five sections. In each section you will find the titles of the chapters from the book *Walking Healed*, with the page number for that chapter. This is to help you journey through the book with the study. It's helpful to read the chapter, then read the lesson and answer the questions. However, if you do not have a copy of *Walking Healed*, you can still do the study. You just won't be able to tackle some of the questions.

As we journey along, you will eventually discover that though there are five sections, each with its own set of Scriptures, they all intertwine just like our lives. God is so amazing in the way He has designed everything and just as our mental, emotional, physical and spiritual states all work together, so do healing, forgiveness, grace, hope, and our purpose.

At the beginning of each section is a memory verse. As you memorize the verse it will help you through the journey through that section. You will also find every memory verse at the back of this workbook. Though I have added only one at the beginning of each section, there are in fact two to three verses for you to memorize throughout your journey. Don't be overwhelmed. This is not a race and there won't be a test. This is for your spiritual growth, lovelies.

> Don't be overwhelmed. This is not a race.

Many of the Scriptures are written out throughout this study, with the questions. However, some verses are just listed so you can look them up in your own Bible. That's called Bible *study*. Have fun with it.

Are you ready for your new walk? Let's get started!

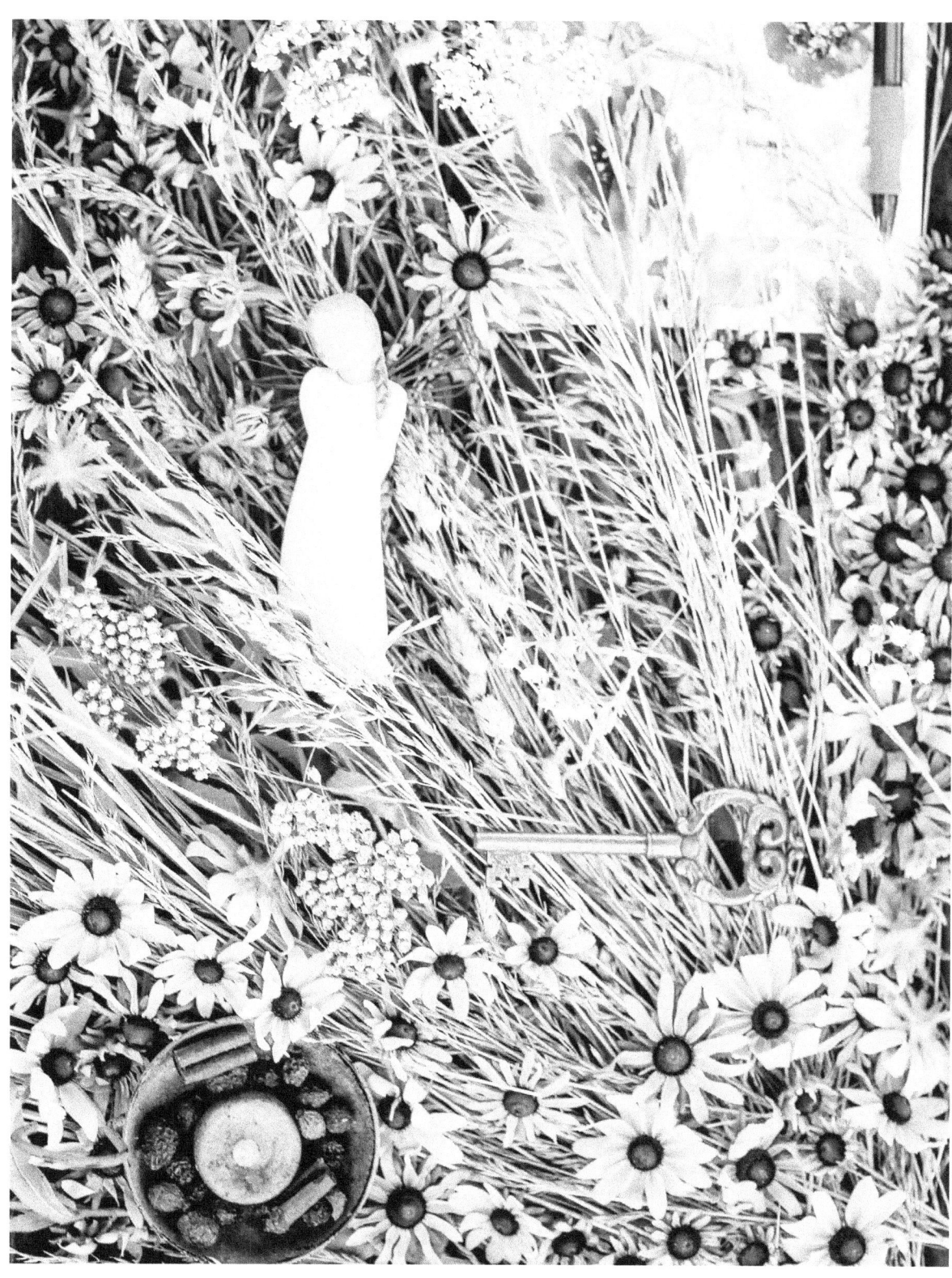

Walking Healed Companion Study

SECTION ONE: HEALING PART ONE – SPIRITUAL

"O LORD, if you heal me, I will be truly healed; if you save me, I will be truly saved. My praises are for you alone!" ~Jeremiah 17:14 (NLT)

Healing comes in many forms. Just as there are many aspects to our lives, there are also many aspects to healing: mental, emotional, physical, and spiritual. We are going to look at how God heals, why, why not, and what our role is in the healing process. Before we do that, we are going to break healing up into two groups: Spiritual and Physical. In Part One we will look at spiritual healing.

First: Know that God is Healer, the Great Physician. He is the Healer of His people. He decides how and when we are healed. Our job is to listen, obey, believe, and receive that healing.

To have a closer, deeper relationship with the Lord, sometimes it's necessary to allow Him to heal us of things that are preventing us from moving up and into our calling, or our purpose. These preventative things are called barriers.

My barriers were depression, intimidation, anxiety, feelings of no self-worth, and very low self-esteem. These were the result of years of verbal and emotional abuse by family and peers.

For others, barriers may be alcohol, drugs, pornography, gambling, fear, or anything that prevents you from operating in the gifts or ministry God is calling you to do.

With spiritual healing comes mental and emotional healing as well. This is where my healing came. Because of years of suffering in depression and intimidation (mental and emotional trauma), my spiritual wellness suffered. I knew God, had accepted Jesus as my Savior, but I couldn't move forward in my relationship with Him because I didn't trust that He wouldn't hurt me as every other person I came in contact did. My belief was skewed. I couldn't trust people so how could I trust God?

Your healing has to come down to making a conscious decision that you want to be healed. You've had enough suffering. It doesn't matter anymore what others might think, you need relief and you need it now. Very often Jesus has to get you to that point that, as a last resort, you'll trust Him to do with you as He pleases because you have nothing more to lose.

It's sad, really, that it takes that drastic of a decision to get you to that place. However, it's not exactly the fault of the one seeking healing. Remember, with mental and emotional trauma and abuse, that person has already been conditioned to believe he or she is not worthy. They are led to believe that their condition is their own fault so no one else can or will help them.

Sadly, as humans we often fall into the category of judging one who is suffering in this capacity when we need to be looking at them through the eyes of Jesus. No one is so far gone that they cannot be helped or healed.

For those who suffer depression, we don't often know why we are going through the things we are. We can't explain the feelings we have or why we do the things we do. Many people don't understand that or the people suffering with it, so they assume the role of trying to help us help ourselves by giving all kinds of advice that simply does not work. Quite often it makes it worse. But these feeling are very real.

Read Romans 12:2 below. There are three parts. First, underline what it says not to do. Second, double underline what it says to do. Third, circle the reason it gives for doing so.

"And do not be conformed to this world, but be transformed by the renewing of your mind, that you may prove what is that good and acceptable and perfect will of God." (NKJV)

What does this say to you?

_____
_____
_____
_____
_____
_____
_____
_____
_____
_____
_____
_____

We may live in the world but we are not of the world. God doesn't want us to conform, to be like the world. He doesn't want us to perform in society or by society's rules. He wants us to trust Him enough to allow Him to transform us into all that He has planned for us. His will for us. Perfection.

Look at the passage again. How do we conform to this world?
_____

Now how can we be transformed instead?
_____

Yet, we have a very real enemy who does not want us to fulfill our journey. He wants to do everything he can to prevent us from becoming all that God designed us to be. He very nearly succeeded in preventing me, to the extreme of beginning his attack on me as a child.

The devil has no idea what God's plans are for you. All he knows is what you *might* become. So he has come to prevent you from succeeding in that, from becoming the person God designed you to be. Because he hates God, he hates you, so he throws everything at you that he knows will affect you, hurt you, and cause you to doubt. Jesus even called the devil what he is, "a liar and the father of it" (John 8:44).

The devil is a thief and will steal everything he can from you if you allow him to.

Read John 10:10 below. In one column write everything the devil has come for. In the next column write what Jesus says He has come for.

"The thief does not come except to steal, and to kill, and to destroy. I have come that they may have life, and that they may have it more abundantly." John 10:10 (NKJV)

The devil	*Jesus*
_____	_____
_____	_____

Which sounds better to you? _____

Knowing that God wants us to renew our minds and be transformed into His perfect will, but also knowing that the devil wants to steal, kill, and destroy God's will for us along with our hopes and dreams, we are now ready to undertake our journey.

Through the pages of *Walking Healed*, I have written about how God healed me and has used me to help others find their way back to their own journey. As you read the chapters designated for each section, prayerfully consider your answers to the questions.

Breaking the Chains (pg. 14)

By trying to please people, you find yourself always in chains, never able to perform enough to gain their approval. They will always bring up your past to keep you in the chains of bondage.

What is the one thing Jesus will never do when you bring everything to Him for healing? _____

The devil wants to keep us in bondage. He will use every means necessary to keep us there, even using people as his way of attacking us.

Who are some of the people he uses?
_____
_____

When the Spirit of the Lord comes upon us, what happens to those chains?
_____

Read Luke 4:18. Even though Jesus spoke these words about Himself, this is also a message and assignment to us from the Lord.

What is the Spirit of the Lord (the Holy Spirit) commissioning us to do? Write each one below.

_____
_____
_____

If you have been healed from something that has controlled your life for a long time, you have been set free and now have a wonderful testimony to share with others. Your chains have been broken, dear one!

God Can Still Use You (pg. 32)

It took me nearly thirty years to figure out that God could still use me despite all the years of depression, intimidation, anxiety and other things I suffered. Many people have a false mindset that they've done too many "bad sins" so they believe that God can't use them. How wrong they are.

In the first part of the chapter, "God Can Still Use You," there is a list of names and the things they were guilty of. *Activity: Below is the mixed up list. Match up the name with the fault below then write how God used each one of these people.*

Person	Fault
Jonah	*Committed adultery*
David	*Had seven demons*
Rahab	*Murderer*
Mary Magdalene	*Prostitute*
Moses	*Ran*

*Jonah*_____

*David*_____

*Rahab*_____

*Mary Magdalene*_____

*Moses*_____

God used these people despite their past. But not once did He ever bring their past up to haunt them once they began serving Him. The same applies to you and me today. Though people will remember, God chooses not to. If we have truly repented, God forgives us and remembers our sins no more.

Look up Hebrews 8:12 and 10:17. What do they say about God and our sins?
_____
_____

If God doesn't remember our sins, what then is separating us from Him?
_____

Read Romans 8:38-39. Can anything separate us from God's love?   Yes or No

Don't look for the approval of others. Focus on the Lord and allow Him to lead you in the direction you need to go. He can still use you and He has great big plans for you.

Take Off Your Mask (pg. 49)

Sometimes our lives become like a masquerade. We have suffered in depression, oppression, intimidation, or maybe even low self-esteem or low confidence for so long that we have a difficult time operating in public. So, we put on a mask to prevent people from seeing the real person inside.

Often, we wear that mask for so long that we even forget who we are. We forget our hopes and dreams because we've lived behind the mask for so long we begin to take on that persona instead of who God made us to be. We live a real life game of charades.

How can we take the mask off and begin to live the life God meant for us to live? We first have to go to Him and seek His forgiveness and healing. In order to do that, we have to admit that we've been living behind a mask. That mask is the lie to the world that there isn't anything wrong with us. It's a lie that we have made others believe, thinking "out of sight, out of mind."

But the battle going on in our minds is what has kept us a prisoner behind the mask we wear. It's time to take off the mask.

Read Isaiah 54:17 (NLT) below. Underline every word that tells you that God is for you.

"But in that coming day no weapon turned against you will succeed. You will silence every voice raised up to accuse you. These benefits are enjoyed by the servants of the LORD; their vindication will come from me. I, the LORD, have spoken."

If you underlined the whole passage you would be correct. God's promise in this passage is that no weapon formed against you will prosper. Every tongue that rises against you will fall. You will enjoy all of God's benefits because they are for you. But not only that, God will vindicate you. To me, that is most exciting! Oh, dear lovelies, we don't have to worry about anything once we have trusted the Lord.

Shields Up! (pg. 60)

When we ask for and receive healing from the Lord, it immediately increases our faith. I experienced this after my own healing, but I hadn't realized it until I experienced a round of spiritual attacks right before a speaking engagement. That's when I realized that it literally felt like I had shields up.

Read Ephesians 6:14-17. List each piece of armor and what it does below. Pay extra close attention to the shield of faith. What does it do?

_____
_____
_____
_____
_____
_____

If we are prepared, if our shields are up, what happens if someone comes along and tries to cause us harm verbally or maybe even physically?

_____
_____

How can we keep our shields up? (pg. 61)

_____

What can we do if we start to feel our shields slipping?

_____
_____
_____

Healing Rain (pg. 65)

After a round of thunderstorms a day earlier, I stood on my porch in a puddle, praising Him for the healing rain He had sent to quench the earth of its thirst. I also learned a lesson that day as well. Continuously talking wasn't allowing me to hear God speak. So I got quiet while holding my Bible close, then realized that maybe He had something to say to me.

I read the following passage out loud that day.

Read it out loud, too. Then write what it says to you on the lines on the next page..

"To You, O Lord, I lift up my soul. O my God, I trust in You; Let me not be ashamed; Let not my enemies triumph over me. Indeed, let no one who waits on You be ashamed; Let those be ashamed who deal treacherously without cause. Show me Your ways, O Lord; Teach me Your paths. Lead me in Your truth and teach me, For You are the God of my salvation; On You I wait all the day. Remember, O Lord, Your tender mercies and Your loving kindnesses, For they are from of old. Do not remember the sins of my youth, nor my transgressions; According to Your mercy remember me, For Your goodness' sake, O Lord." ~Psalm 25:1-7 (NKJV)

Reading God's Word (the Bible) out loud is proclaiming His promises over you. He also reminds us that He hears us. God sees everything and everyone because He is omnipresent. He is everywhere. There is nothing that goes unseen by our awesome God.

When we take everything to Him, we are simply telling Him that we trust Him. In return, He bestows upon us His healing rain. And in that healing rain, we also find freedom.

What is healing rain to you?

Freedom (pg. 68)

Our nation celebrates Independence Day on July fourth. When God heals us, we can celebrate our own independence day of sorts. I celebrate mine on May thirtieth. This is the day that God healed me completely spiritually, mentally, and emotionally. The healing was such an intense experience that there was no way I could deny it, nor could anyone else once they heard my story.

God gives us spiritual freedom when we trust Him and receive the healing that He offers. And just like there were people who didn't like that our country became free, there will be others who don't like that we become spiritually free.

We have to be prepared for such things. God has given us a guideline for that as well.

Read 1 Peter 5:8-9.

The devil is prowling around looking for a way to cause trouble. List the ways we are to handle it.

What reassurance is given, for us to know we are not alone?

_____
_____
_____

Read 1 Peter 5:10 then write it below. What reassurances can you gain from this passage?

_____
_____
_____
_____
_____

Make Up Your Mind (pg. 71)

Every day is a new adventure in our journey. Though we suffer sometimes, He is always there. Many times we ask the question, "If God is so loving then why did He let this happen?" Others may question as well. One thing we have to remember is that God is always for us. He never leaves us. We may not have had our circumstances changed because we refused to trust God and allow Him to work in our lives.

We have to make up our mind to trust Him. We have to stop making excuses and allow God to work in our lives.

An excuse is a lie disguised as a reason.

We give many reasons for the mess we allow ourselves to get into. Whether it's making excuses for the people we allow to bully and abuse us, or whether it's a reason we haven't come to the Lord for help, each reason we give is just a lie the devil gives us to keep us from the abundant life God has for us.

It's time to make up our minds.

Read James 5:12. What does it say about saying "yes" or "no"?

_____
_____

Now look at Jeremiah 29:11. God has a plan for you. Write His plans below.

_____
_____
_____
_____

According to Isaiah 40:31, what happens to those who trust in the Lord?

_____
_____
_____

Got Junk in Your Trunk? (pg. 109)

Are you a collector of junk? Not the lovely treasures we find tucked away in the corner of some antique store. I'm talking about those ugly words that were spoken to you and over you, yesterday, a month ago, or years ago.

The junk we carry for years and years can build up over time, squashed into a little treasure box in the recesses of our minds. They can keep you from living the life God intended for you to live. This is how the enemy makes our lives miserable.

A few pages back we looked at how the enemy prowls around looking for someone to devour. He likes nothing more than to catch you when you're at your weakest moment. He loves to whisper negative, hurtful things into our ears and then watch as we run with it, making a mountain out of a molehill.

But we were never meant to be brought down by those ugly things. We were never meant to carry that junk around in our minds. When the devil whispers lies, we have many ways to defeat him. Let's look at a couple of them.

Look at 2 Corinthians 10:3-6 (NKJV) below.

"For though we walk in the flesh, we do not war according to the flesh. For the weapons of our warfare are not carnal but mighty in God for pulling down strongholds, casting down arguments and every high thing that exalts itself against the knowledge of God, bringing every thought into captivity to the obedience of Christ, and being ready to punish all disobedience when your obedience is fulfilled."

The Apostle Paul says we do not fight a physical (carnal) war. We are fighting a spiritual war. This is how the enemy, the devil gets at us—in our minds.

According to the above passage, what does it say about the weapons of our warfare?

_____

What should we do with the thoughts that are placed in our minds?

_____

_____

Now read Philippians 4:8. List everything we are to think about.

_____
_____
_____

It's an ongoing battle to keep the junk out of our trunk. However, if we obey what Matthew 6:33 says, we will be well on our way to victory!

Write out Matthew 6:33 below.

_____
_____
_____

Short Circuited (pg. 135)

Has your life seemingly short-circuited your faith? Your spiritual belief? It did mine. When I was fifteen, I slipped into a severe state of depression. It was several years before I learned to just live with it. I dealt with it for many years because I got no help. I was never taken to the doctor, only told that I was the only person who could help me. I was led to believe that my situation was my own fault; however, I could never figure out what I did to cause it.

I tried to pray. I tried to trust Jesus. But nothing worked. I was short-circuited. I had unbelief. Because I didn't trust anyone, I couldn't trust Jesus either. My faith was shorted out in the fact that people had let me down in the past; therefore I thought Jesus couldn't help me either.

This short circuitry prevented the Lord from helping me, from Him working His miracles in me. My entire life seemed to have short circuited my belief. It was my unwillingness to trust God to heal me. Though I was a Christian, I still had issues with trust and that was where my wires were shorting out.

Read 2 Peter 1:1(b). When we accept Jesus we are given faith. What reason is given in this passage?
_____
_____

Because of the justice and fairness of Jesus, we have everything we need to operate properly as a child of God. If we are not, we are in a state of unbelief, making us not trust Him for everything.

List some things that might cause us to short circuit our faith.
_____
_____
_____

Now, list some ways we can trust Jesus with our lives so we don't short circuit.
_____
_____
_____

One very important aspect of being short-circuited is that we try to please people instead of pleasing God, which we will discuss in the next section.

Stop People Pleasing (pg. 161)

Are you a people pleaser? Always trying to make things right with everyone so no one feels left out or unhappy, people pleasers wears themselves out making sure everyone is happy while they themselves are miserable. It's no way to live.

If you are a people pleaser, you will waste your time, maybe even years, trying to satisfy the very people who can never be satisfied. Let me encourage you: it is not your place to satisfy them. The only thing that can satisfy a restless soul is Jesus.

Read Luke 1:46-47, 49 from the Amplified Bible. Let it speak to your heart and soul.

Then rewrite it in your own words, in the space below it.

"My soul magnifies and extols the Lord, And my spirit rejoices in God my Savior… For He Who is almighty has done great things for me—and holy is His name…"

_____
_____

How does that speak to you today?

_____
_____
_____

What "great things" has He done for you? List them below.

_____
_____
_____

Pleasing the Lord is not difficult. He is our Audience of One. If we doubt, seek His advice. He is always on hand to offer guidance without shaming us. God loves us so much, dear ones is there any reason we should doubt that?

Look at 1 Thessalonians 4:1(a) from the NLT. "Finally, dear brothers and sisters, we urge you in the name of the Lord Jesus to live in a way that pleases God…"

What a great encouragement. Even in God's Word, letters from those who have gone before us, thousands of years before us, even, are encouraging us to live in a way that pleases God. It doesn't say to please others. Only God.

He is always listening to you, for you, watching out for you, and always ready to bless you. Today, stop trying to please others and look to God. You don't have to perform for Him. He already knows what you're all about and He's crazy about you.

Healing: Part Two - Physical

This section is a lot shorter than the previous section, yet the two go together like peas and carrots.

In this section, we will take what God's Word says about healing to a new level. We will look at the healing miracles of Jesus and how we may apply those to our lives. Before we do, though, I have a small confession to make.

You may be wondering why I'm talking about physical healing when I've been very adamant about how God healed me mentally, emotionally, and spiritually. Honestly, He did heal me in those three areas. But it was long before that that God gave me a physical healing which began my journey to find healing for my mind and spirit.

In November of 2005 we had moved to a very tiny home in the country. We had sold our motorcycle and bought four-wheelers to ride out in the field and through the woods with our teenage son. It was a good move all the way around. At least it was until I got hurt.

I had gone riding with my son and my brother one afternoon. We rode out through some woods around our city lake. Over fallen trees, through deep ruts, through mud and water we rode, having the time of our lives. Back and forth we went for hours. Then my son and I rode home. When I got off my four-wheeler my back was stiff.

I remember thinking, boy that's going to hurt tomorrow. And it did. My lower back was sore from riding. But in my mind, it was no big deal, just a sore back. I thought I had pulled muscles that I hadn't used in a very long time. I had just turned forty so it was expected that I begin having physical aches, right?

After a couple of weeks, though, the pain hadn't lessened. Instead it had grown worse. It continued to get worse and worse over the next couple of months, too. It got so bad that I could barely get in and out of bed or in and out of the car to drive my son to school.

Painkillers didn't work. Heat or ice didn't work. It kept escalating to the point that I began walking hunched over because I couldn't straighten up. I had gone to a chiropractor who twisted and turned me, popped me this way and that, only to go home in tears because the pain was so excruciating that I couldn't even sit without crying.

My medical doctor gave me strong pain meds to kill the pain. They didn't work. All they did was cause me extreme nausea and make me sleep. The pain never went away. As the doctor continued to increase the dosage of my pain meds, the pain in my back increased as well. With that, my nerves got worse and worse, too.

I would go to church only to have to leave services and lay in a classroom until the end of services and pray that God would just let me die so I could get some relief. Obviously it wasn't His plan to take me Home because I'm still here.

After about three months of pain and anguish another chiropractor approached me. I wasn't aware that we went to church together. He came to me and said, "I've been watching you for weeks and it kills me to see you in such pain." He then invited me to come to his office because he was confident that he could help me. I was skeptical. I had already been to a chiropractor with no relief. He assured me that he would not hurt me, but he knew in his heart that he could help me if I would just trust him.

So I went.

By this time, I was in excruciating physical pain and the medication I was on had damaged my nerves and caused me to slip into the most severe state of depression, panic, and anxiety that I had ever been in in my entire life. However, this chiropractor, true to his word, never hurt me one time.

He took X-rays and discovered a birth defect in my lower back was causing curvature of the spine. When I had been riding that day several months earlier, in the jarring, twisting and bouncing on the four-wheeler I had flattened a disc between two vertebrae and they had pinched my sciatic nerve which was causing all my pain. In that pinched nerve, I also had nerve damage down my left leg and had no feeling in it. This was news to me because the pain in my back was so severe I had no idea that my leg was numb.

I was put through adjustments three times a week along with decompression therapy and heat therapy. Decompression therapy is buckling you in a couple of harnesses on a table and allowing a machine to gently stretch you, thereby alleviating pressure on the area where your trouble is. Mine was in my lower back. By stretching my back, it was giving that disc a chance to unflatten, which would in turn move those vertebrae back into place and relieve the pressure on my sciatic nerve.

I've said all that to say this: God worked through that chiropractor for more than a year to heal me physically. I went through lots of therapy, tears, and bouts of anxiety attacks while being treated in the chiropractor's office, and through it all, God ministered to me through the chiropractor and his staff. While crying on the adjustment table, my chiropractor prayed over me while he worked on me. He ministered to me, assuring me that one day I would be pain free. Not long afterward, he was right. And one of the greatest blessings is, he never charged me a dime. He told me that he saw the ministry my family was in and because he didn't think he had much talent, this was his way of giving back to God's Kingdom, by keeping His kids healthy so they can do their ministry.

How far will God go to get your attention? If He'll give His only Son to die for us, you can bet He'll go to any extreme necessary to bring one of His children back to Him.

It took over a year to get my back straight again with very little pain. I still have to watch what I do, but it's a small reminder of how far God went to begin my healing process. It was another six years before I came to the place where He would heal me mentally, emotionally, and spiritually.

Maybe you're wondering what all this has to do with anything pertaining to this book. Let me encourage you today by saying whatever you are going through, God is bigger than any of it. If we look to Him and allow Him to lead us and minister to us, to teach us and reach us, we will learn that the things we are going through are minute in comparison with eternity.

The things we experience in this life can all be used to reach someone else who is going through what we have. We have a testimony to share with others, showing them the love of God and His healing touch.

In talking about healing, it often scares some people because they don't understand. "Why do we need healing?" and "How do we get healed?" are a couple of questions that float around those who are curious, yet still unsure about stepping forward.

Why do we need healing? Because we often live in our misery without accessing the healing God has to offer. Another reason is because we simply cannot do it on our own. "Heal thyself" seems to be the statement of society. If I eat right, exercise, use essential oils, contort my body, pack the mud on, stand on my head at three thirty in the afternoon, whatever the latest fad is, then I'll heal myself and don't need help from anyone.

While this sounds extreme, the point is that we often try all kinds of fads and fashions to make ourselves thinner, more beautiful, younger, and anything that seems to work to make us feel better about ourselves. We'll use if it means we'll be healed and live longer. The truth is that our health, youth, and very life depend on God. It's His decision how, when, where, and why to heal us. No, He doesn't want us to suffer. However, if our suffering will lead to reaching someone for Him, He allows us to go through some difficult situations in order to bring glory to Himself.

So, how do we "get healed?" The answer is simple and yet complex at the same time. Simply put, the answer is, *ask*. All we have to do to be healed is to ask God to heal us. The more detailed answer is found by digging deeper into God's Word and actually participating with Him, seeking His help.

Let's look at James 5:14-15 in the NKJV. What does it say we are to do? Underline it.
"Is anyone among you sick? Let him call for the elders of the church, and let them pray over him, anointing him with oil in the name of the Lord. And the prayer of faith will save the sick, and the Lord will raise him up. And if he has committed sins, he will be forgiven."

What does it say about people praying over you if you're sick?
_____
_____
_____
_____

The use of anointing oil is significant in that it has been used since the beginning of time. Throughout the Old and New Testaments, oil was prominent in the religious life of ancient Israelites. It could anoint objects, spaces, kings, priests, or worshipers could use it for offerings. It also fueled the lampstands in the temple.

Read the following passages and list the ways anointing oil was used.
    Exodus 29:7 _____
    Leviticus 8:12 _____

1 Samuel 16:13 _____

Mark 6:13 _____

Anointing oil in many ways is used to bless the one being anointed. As people are anointed with oil, not only are they blessed, they are usually being prayed for, commissioned by the Lord, given a prophetic Word, and even being filled with the Holy Spirit. Many times, sick people are healed while being anointed with oil **(refer back to James 5:14-15 and Mark 6:13).**

In regard to physical ailments or emotional ones, one thing that happens when we begin to have trouble is we isolate ourselves. It's not good for us to be alone. When we begin to have issues the first thing we need to do is call for the elders of the church.

Who are the elders of the church?

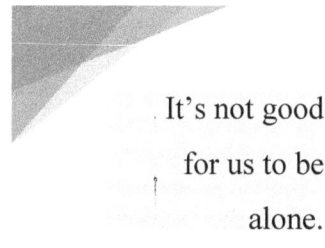

It's not good for us to be alone.

They can be anyone who stands in a leadership role in your church; deacons, sometimes called elders, prayer warriors, associate pastors, core leaders, teachers, etc. Anyone who holds a leadership role or a very respected role in the church is considered an elder. This is a person whom you know to be in tune with the Holy Spirit, who is a mighty prayer person, or even has Godly wisdom. Some churches are very specific about elders, deacons, leaders, etc. Utilize the leadership in your church as you are encouraged or led.

Go to them. These people are placed in your life for a reason. They can, will, and want to make things better for you. Just as James 5 states, if we are sick, whether it's physical, mental, emotional, or spiritual, we are to call on the elders of the church and ask them to pray for us.

Make a conscious and deliberate decision that you want to be healed, regardless of your situation. Decide. Don't back down. Don't give up. Go boldly to God and ask. Ask. Then receive the healing.

Read Psalm 142:1-2 (NLT).

"I cry out to the LORD; I plead for the LORD's mercy. I pour out my complaints before him and tell him all my troubles."

What does this Psalm give us permission to do?
_____

Now read Lamentations 3:36 (NLT).
"You heard me when I cried, "Listen to my pleading! Hear my cry for help!"

Does God hear us when we cry out to Him? Yes or No?

What does it take to be healed? _____

    Jesus healed many different people during His ministry. Men, women and children came to Him. Some were even brought to him because they couldn't come on their own. Some people even came to Jesus who had been shunned by society. He healed them all.

Let's look at one in particular. Read John 5:1-9.

    Jesus came to the pool of Bethesda where people went to be healed in the pool. But He went to a man He knew had been lame (unable to walk) for thirty-eight years.

What did Jesus ask the man at the pool of Bethesda? _____

What was the man's reply?
_____
_____

Why do you suppose the man answered Jesus in this way? Was he making excuses for himself or do you think he truly wanted to be healed but couldn't figure out a way to get in the pool?

_____

_____

_____

Jesus asked the man, "Would you like to get well?" It's a yes or no answer. Do you really want healing? That's what He asks us all today. Do you *really* want it? If you do, what are you willing to do to get healed?

Sadly, many say they want healed, even come forward for prayer and allow the elders to pray over them. Yet, as soon as they walk out the doors they go right back into their old habits and illnesses. It's sad to say, some like the pity and attention that their issues bring. They may say they want healed but truly believe that the attention would go away if that happened.

You have to have faith, believing and receiving and do not doubt, in order to be healed. You actually have to make an effort.

Read James 1:6 (NKJV). What does it say we are not to do?

_____

When we doubt we are saying that we don't trust the Lord. Doubting is unbelief, plain and simple. Whether we would like to admit it or not, when we go to the Lord in prayer, asking for healing we must believe that He hears us and that He heals us. That's why it is very important to make a conscious and deliberate decision that we want to be healed.

It's so much easier to ask for and receive healing from the Lord when we have decided that's what we want. He knows our hearts therefore it's easy for Him to answer us because He knows if we are sincere in our asking or if we have doubt and fear when we come to Him with our requests. Just as James 1:6 says, we are to go to Him with no doubting. If we doubt we are like the waves of the sea, being tossed to and fro. How can we expect to receive anything from the Lord then?

When we make up our minds that we want healing we often get focused on that and nothing can stop us; not even a crowd of people.

Read Luke 8:43-48.

What did Jesus tell the woman after He healed her? _____
What had made her well? _____

With healing, sometimes the results are seen immediately (my situation with spiritual healing). Sometimes the results take a little while to manifest (show up). It depends on your circumstances. God may need to move you or He may need to move something or someone who is blocking you.

What types of things or people could block you from a healing from the Lord? (I've added one to help get you started).
A negative attitude or person

_____
_____
_____
_____

How do you know you've been healed? Read the following Scriptures then write the answer to this question on the lines next to each one.

Isaiah 53:5 and 1 Peter 2:24 _____
John 14:13 _____
Mark 5:34 _____
Jeremiah 17:14 _____

Is it a sin to have depression, anxiety, or a physical ailment? No. Staying in it when you've been healed *is*. Healing whether mental, emotional, spiritual or physical is not about feelings. It's all about faith in Jesus.

A Time of Prayer

The Lord loves it when we come to Him in prayer. He especially loves when we incorporate His word in our prayer time. Choose a Scripture from the lessons or memory verse and write a prayer of healing in the space provided. Let it come from your heart.

Walking Healed Companion Study

SECTION TWO: FORGIVENESS

Part One – Forgiveness for Others

"If you forgive those who sin against you, your heavenly Father will forgive you. But if you refuse to forgive others, your Father will not forgive your sins."
~Matthew 6:14-15 (NLT)

In our last couple of lessons we have learned that healing changes things. Once we receive healing, whether spiritual, physical, or both, we instantly know that everything is different. Our lives are no longer the same. Healing elevates us to a whole other level. We've been raised up, we need to step up.

When you find healing, you'll find forgiveness. Forgiveness also has two parts: Forgiveness for others, and forgiveness for yourself. We are going to look at forgiveness for others first.

Forgiveness for Others

Something we need to remember and get in our beautiful little heads is that this is not our fight. No matter how much we want to believe that it is, it's simply not our fight. This fight belongs to the Lord. The next thing we need to realize is that Jesus forgave. We are to do likewise. We may not see it that way (at first) because we look at things from the natural and not the supernatural; from the outside not the inside, the head and not the heart.

It may be difficult for us to grasp, but when we've been wronged by someone, whether it's family, a friend, a co-worker, someone from church, or random person out in public, this is not about you. It's not personal. It's spiritual. It sounds crazy, doesn't it? But that person or group of people, no matter how much it seems like they have targeted you, have no earthly idea that what they are doing is being a ploy by the devil to get at your Creator.

Think about that one for just a bit. I'll wait…

…Okay, let's move on. If you look back in the Old Testament, even back to the Garden of Eden, you'll see that the devil has been behind attacks on God's people. Whether it was to get permission from God Himself to test their faith as he did with Job, or whether it was just to place evil in the hearts of people who were enemies of God's people, Satan has been "patrolling the earth, watching everything that's going on" (Job 1:7b NLT). Whether he attacks on his own or at the permission from God to test our faith is irrelevant. The fact is that he's patrolling. He's watching. He's waiting to try and make a mess of things for us by his own means or by using someone to cause us harm.

This brings us to forgiveness. No matter what has happened in your life or mine, Jesus commands us to forgive. Once we find healing we can't stay where we once were. We have to move out of our box. Healing opens the doors for us to see, find, and extend forgiveness to others; especially to those who have hurt us the most.

Forgiveness is not passive. It's assertive. It's aggressive. I had posted this statement one evening in a quote on Facebook. I was promptly questioned by someone asking, "Exactly what does that mean? Forgiveness is assertive, aggressive. What is assertive aggressive forgiveness?" Here's my response:

Being assertive is standing up for your rights while still respecting the rights of others. Forgiving assertively is like that; respectful of both you and the one you're forgiving. But by being aggressive in forgiveness, you often have to take a defensive (or offensive) role in forgiving some people (and sometimes yourself) whenever it's a big effort to do so (like when you really don't want to because of the level of hurt involved). But forgiveness is never passive because if it was, you'd never do it.

Forgiving others also doesn't mean restoration, acceptance, or even justification. Forgiveness means a reconciliation of sorts, taking your offender out of your hands and placing them in the hands of God. Forgiving others is not letting that person off the hook. It's letting *you* off the hook.

I said earlier that Jesus commands us to forgive. Look at the passage below. What does Jesus say about forgiveness?

"If you forgive those who sin against you, your heavenly Father will forgive you. But if you refuse to forgive others, your Father will not forgive your sins." Matthew 6:14-15 (NLT)

_____

_____

It is not your place to be judge, jury, and executioner. Our battle is not really ours. It belongs to the Lord.

Read 2 Chronicles 20:15 and Proverbs 21:31. What do both of these passages say?
_____

By forgiving others, you have reconciliation of the *issue*. The *relationship* with that person however, does not go back to the way things were. It never does. The relationship is forever altered. You may also have to keep your distance.

You can forgive without confrontation. However, if you know the other person will confront and attack you, then forgive from a distance and move on. Save yourself from further harm; physical, emotional, verbal, and spiritual. To forgive and move on may be the toughest thing you do.

How many times do we forgive? In Matthew 18:21-22, Peter asked Jesus how often we should forgive someone who sins against us. Then he asks, "Seven times?" (vs 21).

Look at Jesus' answer in the verse below.
"No, not seven times," Jesus replied, "but seventy times seven!"

Does that mean that we are to forgive others only four hundred-ninety times? No. It's a metaphor. Jesus means that we are to forgive others indefinitely. Jesus does. It just doesn't mean to allow your offender to keep abusing or hurting you.

The greatest act of forgiveness:

"Father, forgive them. For they know not what they do." ~Jesus (Luke 23:34, KJV)

Pattern your forgiveness after His.

In the following chapters, there are many ways to find and extend forgiveness. Sometimes things work out. Others times they don't. No matter how circumstances turn out, always know that God has your best interest at hand if you will only trust Him and allow Him to work things out according to His plan.

Mending Fences (pg. 17)

Forgiveness is part of our journey. It's a journey in itself to forgive others. Whether they choose to forgive you is on them. You can't make people forgive you and sadly, some don't want to. Many never will forgive and will continue to cause issues and division among us.

In our journey it's about forgiving others. Forgiveness is how we mend our fences with those around us and find happiness within ourselves. Deep inside each of us we all have a longing to be able to have peace with everyone, whether it's doable or not.

There are people in your life who have caused division. Everyone has someone like that, maybe more than one. Sadly, these are the people that we simply cannot be around. No matter how much we love them, if they are continually causing you grief, hurt, and always finding some way to ridicule you, hurt you, or laugh at you, then you must make the difficult decision to separate yourself from them.

Read Romans 16:17-18 (NKJV) below.

"Now I urge you, brethren, note those who cause divisions and offenses, contrary to the doctrine which you learned, and avoid them. For those who are such do not serve our Lord Jesus Christ, but their own belly, and by smooth words and flattering speech deceive the hearts of the simple."

Whom does it say we are to avoid? _____
Whom do these people serve? _____
How do they deceive us? _____

How then are we supposed to reconcile or mend our fences with those who have hurt us? There will be those in our lives that we know we can go to and be able to talk things through, thereby mending our differences. However, there will also be people in our lives whom we know, that when we go to them with our concerns or hurt, will only retaliate in a negative way, making things worse and bringing up the past which causes more hurt. These are the people we will have to sever ties with.

When we consult with the Lord before we confront someone who has hurt us, He will direct us in the way we should go.

Look at Matthew 18:15. How does it say we are to handle someone who has hurt us?
_____
_____

There will also be times when you absolutely know that the person who has hurt you will not receive what you have to say. This person may take your confrontation and use it against you. They may twist your words and throw them back at you, making you the guilty person, saying it was actually you who said the ugly words and it was you who hurt them. You have to be on your guard so that you do not become victimized again. You must then turn them over to the Lord and let Him deal with them. This is when you must accept that you cannot do anything to make things right with that person.

The hardest thing for me to do was to pray for those in my life who are this way. But you must forgive. I had to forgive. Dear lovelies, you have to get to that point. Having others pray for me is what helped break through years of hurt and oppression. God released me of it. He will release you, too.

The devil will keep you down any way he can to keep you from mending fences, whether it's with others or within yourself, or even with the Lord.

Read 1 Peter 5:8-9 (HCSB) below.

"Be serious! Be alert! Your adversary the Devil is prowling around like a roaring lion, looking for anyone he can devour. Resist him and be firm in the faith, knowing that the same sufferings are being experienced by your fellow believers throughout the world."

The passage tells us two very important things right off. What are they?
_____
What is the devil constantly doing? _____
Who is he looking for? _____
What does it say we are to do? _____
What else are we to know? _____

You are not alone. Did you get that? You. Are. Not. Alone! God made sure that we would never be alone in our journey. You have people all around you who are going through, or who have gone through the same things as you. Those who have not gone through it will not understand. Those of you seeking to find what I did will find it.

Offense and Defense (pg. 21)

Whenever someone questions you or confronts you on any issue, do you become defensive? Do you sit and analyze what just happened, going through several scenarios as to how you could have done things differently? Maybe it's time to stop the mindless wandering and learn how to forgive others as Christ has forgiven you.

"And forgive us our debts, as we forgive our debtors." ~Matthew 6:12 (NKJV)

Once the chains are broken, we need to get rid of them so that the remaining pieces don't collect to form another way to keep us in bondage (slavery). The enemy will use what's left to remind us of past hurts, which causes us get defensive easily. He will remind us of how we handled things in the past. But dear one, don't get defensive and definitely don't get offended.

Read the passage below, then answer the questions with an open mind.

"Christ has liberated us to be free. Stand firm then and don't submit again to a yoke of slavery." ~Galatians 5:1 (HCSB)

What do you think it means to be liberated? _____
How are we to stand? _____

If we stand firm, not giving in to the pressures the enemy, or others put on us, we will walk in the victory Jesus gave us when He defeated death, hell, and the grave. We will walk in freedom when we stand in confidence of the healing He gives us.

Read 1 Thessalonians 5:17 and write it below:

_____

When we get into God's Word (the Bible), read, and pray, we are standing firm against the pressures and the confrontations of the enemy. In the passage above it says to "pray without ceasing." How exactly to do we do that? It's very simple.

Whenever negative or oppressive thoughts creep into your mind, recognize them for what they are: an attack of the enemy. That's when you counter-attack with God's Word. Recite out loud what His Word says. This is praying without ceasing.

Also, a resounding "NO!" spoken out loud will stop the negative thoughts from having a rerun inside your mind.

Look at James 4:7-8(a) (NLT) below.
"So humble yourselves before God. Resist the devil, and he will flee from you. Come close to God, and God will come close to you."

First of all, what does it say we are to do? _____
What happens when we resist the devil? _____
When we come close to God, what does He do? _____

You must know that God is just waiting for us to come to Him. The enemy only has the power that you give to him. He cannot do anything on his own to overpower you. So don't give him any power. Dear lovelies, we have more power in the tips of our little finger than the devil does in his whole body.

Whenever you begin to have those crippling thoughts, say out loud, No! You have to stand up for yourself both in the flesh and in the spirit. Take back your life. Hand it over to God.

Read Ephesians 6:13 (NKJV) below.

"Therefore take up the whole armor of God that you may be able to withstand in the evil day, and having done all, to stand."

Whenever you have your armor on, you can and will stand up to the devil and anyone else who comes against you. Whenever you memorize God's Word, hiding it in your heart (Psalm 119:11), you will have the power to overcome those who try to bring up past mistakes. None of that matters anymore. Let Him be your defense and never be offended again. It's part of your journey to forgiveness.

Get Rid of Your "BUT!" (pg. 29)

When God heals you of all the stuff weighing you down; depression, oppression, unforgiveness, bitterness, and whatever else you're harboring, He will also begin working on your "but."

When you harbor ill thoughts for a long period of time, it begins to weigh heavily on you. It drags you down and keeps you from becoming who God wants you to be. Maybe you feel justified. However, those thoughts will manifest into a lie that disguises itself as "the right thing to do."

Look at the quote from* Walking Healed *below:
"You may be saying, "I understand that, "but" it's just too hard!"

When we begin to reason with ourselves and others, justifying our actions and why we feel the way we do, we are only dabbling in whatever it is that we don't want to get rid of. We always add a "but" to the equation to justify ourselves.

This is how we give the enemy power to control us. So what can we do to eliminate that? Get rid of our but.

Read the following passage out of John 21:20-22 (NKJV).

"Then Peter, turning around, saw the disciple whom Jesus loved following, who also had leaned on His breast at the supper, and said, "Lord, who is the one who betrays You?" Peter, seeing him, said to Jesus, "But Lord, what about this man?"

Jesus said to him, "If I will that he remain till I come, what is that to you? You follow Me."

Peter, John, and Jesus are walking together and Jesus is giving Peter his assignment. However, Peter looks back at John and what is the first word he says? _____

What were the last three little words that Jesus said to Peter?

_____ _____ _____

Isn't it just like us today? We know what God wants us to do. We even hear Him speak through His word and even into our hearts. Yet the first word we come back with is, "But."

How can we have forgiveness for others whenever we stay in a continuous state of but? We have to get rid of our but and move forward.

Look back on page 31 of Walking Healed. What is the only thing holding you back?
_____

Let's move on.

Past is Past (pg. 46)

When Jesus saves us, we are a completely new person. God remembers our past no more. Sadly, many people choose to remember our past and try to bring it back up.

Look at Psalm 103:12 from the HSCB.

"As far as the east is from the west, so far has He removed our transgressions from us."

Exactly how far are our sins (transgressions) removed from us? _____
_____

People like to remember. God, on the other hand, chooses to forget. Why? Because He is God and He is Love, so of course He is going to forgive and forget. How sad a life and a future we would have had He chosen not to forget. What good would that do?

To God, if we have asked Him to forgive us, it's forgotten. The past is in the past.

Read 2 Corinthians 5:17-18, then answer the questions below.
If we are in Christ, what have we become? _____
What has passed? _____
What task or ministry has God given us? _____

If God has given us the task, or ministry, of reconciliation, I think He was serious when He told us to forgive others. How can we do that if we are constantly bringing up everyone's past? It's time to leave the past in the past.

Setting Boundaries (pg. 57)

When we give in to fear, we allow it to come in and control our lives. It builds a fortress around us preventing us from confronting and taking charge of situations that we allow people to place us in. We thereby live in a constant state of oppression, causing people to have little respect for us because we don't stand up for ourselves.

Look back at page 39 of this study to Romans 16:17-18. Who does it say to watch out for? _____

What does it say we are to do? _____

By avoiding divisive, controlling people, or people who continually cause problems for us, we are not prolonging the inevitable which would be a negative confrontation or avoiding the truth. We are simply setting boundaries.

By distancing yourself from said people it often causes them to lash out at you more. However, by staying away from them, you have set your boundaries.

Look at page 58 of* Walking Healed*. In the space provided, list what your boundaries say to those you are keeping your distance from.

1. _____
2. _____
3. _____

Do not be afraid to stand up for yourself. Do it in a loving way. Before you remove yourself from others, please make sure they know where you stand. Also remember that you know the people in your life better than anyone. Sometimes, to confront those who oppress you only causes more issues for you. Always put Christ first and trust Him to help you through your situations. Pray first, then let the Holy Spirit guide you and give you the words to say.

Set your boundaries regardless of how others treat you. The Lord will back you up.

Wisdom in Reconciling (pg. 77)

When God heals, He restores. A great weight is lifted from within. Not only will you truly feel forgiven, but you will be able to feel forgiveness for others. I know that I did. Yet, what about down the road when you face your oppressors again? What do you do? How do you stay honest, yet maintain your integrity?

It's very important that you seek the wisdom of the Holy Spirit before opening your mouth. Don't go into a confrontation with a self-righteous attitude. We know there are people in our lives who are going to cause issues.

Read the passage below.

"But the wisdom from above is first pure, then peace-loving, gentle, compliant, full of mercy and good fruits, without favoritism and hypocrisy." ~James 3:17 (HCSB)

List everything this passage says that wisdom is.
_____
_____

Now, list everything wisdom is without. _____
_____

When we focus on God's wisdom and the godly wisdom He gives us, we can invoke a peaceable reaction to those who seek confrontation.

List the three ways we can react to show someone who tries to intimidate us that we aren't going to fight with them (pg. 78):

1. _____
2. _____
3. _____

Sometimes that will be enough to diffuse the situation, though sometimes our intimidators are looking for a fight. Other times, reconciliation with someone just does not happen. Still, seek God's wisdom.

Look at James 1:5-6(a) in the NKJV below.

"If any of you lacks wisdom, let him ask of God, who gives to all liberally and without reproach, and it will be given to him, But let him ask in faith, with no doubting..."

How does God give and to whom?
_____
_____

How are we to ask God? _____

What does it say that God will do when we ask Him for wisdom? _____
_____

When we go to God boldly with our requests, He answers us. But we are to have faith and do not doubt. God will do what He says He will. Just trust Him and wait patiently on Him.

When Friendships Fail (pg. 80)

Restoring relationships is a difficult adventure. Many times we cannot restore one, and we just have to move on, continuing in prayer for the one who will not be moved.

It does not settle things to continually drag up the past, trying to get over it. Yet many times, the people we surround ourselves with thrive on the past mistakes of others, taking great pleasure in dwelling on the negative, keeping us in a constant state of strife.

This bears repeating; In order to be forgiven, we must also forgive.

Even when friendships fail because of un-forgiveness, we still must move forward and allow God to heal us, continuing in prayer for the friend we lost due to the other's unwillingness to reconcile.

Let's look a group of passages to see how the Lord handles both sides of the situation.

Read Psalm 138:3.

What happens as soon as we pray? _____

How does the Lord encourage us? _____

Now read verse 6.

Who does God care for? _____

Who does He keep His distance from? _____

Now look at the first part of verse 7 below.

"Though I am surrounded by troubles, you will protect me from the anger of my enemies.

What does God protect us from? _____

Notice that the question asks, what, and not who. God protects us from the anger of our enemies.

Now read the rest of the verse below.

"You reach out your hand, and the power of your right hand saves me."

What is in His right hand? _____

What does it do? _____

I've taken more time with this chapter because I believe we all deal with the anger of our enemies. Sadly, many of our now enemies were once friends who, by some unfortunate events have now declared their un-forgiveness toward us. Or maybe it's the other way around. Whatever the case may be God knows about it and is dealing with both sides accordingly. Which side do you find yourself on?

Look at Ephesians 4:32 (NLT) below.

"Instead, be kind to each other, tenderhearted, forgiving one another, just as God through Christ has forgiven you."

What does this passage tell us we are to do? _____
_____

How are we to do it? _____

Forgive as God through Christ forgave us. We may not be able to reconcile friendships, but we can be kind. We can be tenderhearted and forgiving, if only from a distance. When you've forgiven, you have done your part. Continuing to pray for that person is the only thing that you can continue to do. You have taken your hands off and out of the situation and allowed the Lord to take over. And that's really all we are required to do.

Learning to Let Go (pg. 93)

I often hear people say things like, "I'm not very good at letting go of thing," or "I haven't mastered the art of releasing the past." Do you wonder how they can possibly have forgiveness in their hearts? They don't. You can talk all day, saying you've forgiven but the truth is that if you can't talk about it without getting upset or angry, then you haven't really let go of it.

Look at a comparison of forgiving and letting go in Matthew 18:21-35
What did the king do with the first servant who owed him "millions of dollars?"
_____

What happened when the man left the king? _____
_____

When the king found out what happened, how did he handle it? _____
_____

How many times did Jesus tell Peter we are to forgive? _____
What does that say to you about forgiveness? _____
_____

Forgiveness is simply deciding to cancel a debt. It doesn't mean that we let the one who hurt us off the hook. It just means that we decided we aren't going to hold a grudge against those who have caused us pain. It also doesn't mean that these people are innocent.

When we choose forgiveness, choose to let go of the wrongs done to us, we can pray for these people, handing them over to the Lord. We then give him room to work on our behalf. Remember, in our earlier lessons, the battle is not ours. It belongs to God. Choosing to forgive others actually releases us from the chains of bondage, not them.

Zombies…the Walking Wounded (pg. 177)

Being hurt by others is not fun. It causes scars. It also causes us to walk around wounded, hence…a zombie. Sometimes we think there is no end in sight for us when we walk around for so long wounded by others, shuffling, snarling, moaning, growling, and hurting others.

Read Psalm 34:15, 17 from the NLT.

"The eyes of the LORD watch over those who do right; his ears are open to their cries for help… The LORD hears his people when they call to him for help, He rescues them from all their troubles."

The eyes of the Lord are always watching over His children. If you belong to the Lord, you can bet He sees you, dear lovely one. He hasn't forgotten you.

What does it say about the Lord's eyes and ears? _____
_____
When we call to the Lord for help, does He hear us? _____
What else does it say He does? _____
_____
How many of our troubles does He rescue us from? _____

In the original Greek and Hebrew the translation for the word "all" is the same. All means ***ALL***! So when God's Word says that He rescues us from all our troubles that means *every single trouble* we have or will have. All we have to do is cry to Him for help.

It's kind of like a fairy tale. We cry for help and our Knight in Shining Armor comes riding in and rescues us. He is always listening, always watching, always waiting. All we have to do is receive it.

We may go through life with scars, but Jesus makes them something beautiful to use to help heal other zombies.

Look at Psalm 118:17 and Psalm 147:3 from the Amplified Bible, then write how it says He heals us.

"I shall not die but live, and shall declare the works and recount the illustrious acts of the Lord." ~Psalm 118:17

"He heals my broken heart and binds up my wounds [curing my pains and sorrows]." ~Psalm 147:3

How does He heal us? _____
_____

Once we are healed, we really can use our scars to help other people. Rather than allow the enemy to keep us in misery, we can allow Jesus to pluck the bitterness out of us and move us forward.

What does 1 Peter 3:10-11 say we should do if we want to enjoy life and see many happy days? _____
_____

Be a survivor, dear lovely ones instead of a wounded zombie!

Unlocking Your Door (pg. 188)

Our weakness is the key to God's strength. It's the key to unlock the door to whatever it is that God is calling you to do. Once unlocked though, you must open the door and walk through.

Look at what God says to Paul in 2 Corinthians 12:9(a) (NKJV).
"And He said to me, "My grace is sufficient for you, for My strength is made perfect in weakness."

His grace is truly all we need. But what else does He say in the latter part of that?
_____

We may think we are too weak to walk through, but if we'll trust Him to help us, He will walk us through everything we face.

We are called to forgive others. Through our trials, hardship, and negative things in our lives, we get pitted. Sometimes we feel too weak to show forgiveness to anyone. It's at that moment that our weakness opens up the door for God to show His mercy and forgiveness through us. We just have to step through.

Shift your focus. Don't focus on your weakness. Let it unlock the door to whatever it is that God has for you just beyond that. You may find something very beautiful.

On the lines below, write a prayer of forgiveness for those who have hurt you. Be as specific as you can. God knows your heart. Give it all up and give it all to Him and let Him fight your battle. It's time to let it go.

Forgiveness: Part Two – Forgiveness for Yourself

Forgiving is difficult enough sometimes. But sometimes we find ourselves in the situation that we must forgive ourselves. Not everyone's forgiveness story is the same. Being forgiven, though, does not mean things get easier for us. Many times they get more difficult.

Not everyone practices forgiveness. Some people simply refuse to forgive. There are also times when the enemy sees an opportunity to bring up things from our past that caused us great shame, so he uses that against us to cause us to beat ourselves up once more.

We can't walk around with the mentality, "I can't forgive myself." In doing so, we are telling God that Jesus' death on the cross was not enough. But in Psalm 103:12 it states that He has removed our sins from us "as far as the east is from the west." It's time we do ourselves a favor and forgive ourselves.

Do Yourself a Favor (pg. 106)

Nowhere else in the Bible is there a passage about forgiving ourselves. It's just not in there. Let's look at what is in there though.

Read Hebrews 8:12 (NLT)
After He forgives our wickedness (our sins), what does He say He will do? _____
_____

If God never remembers our sins, how can we continue to beat ourselves up over them? It's an attack of the enemy.

Look at the passage below:
"If we confess our sins, He is faithful and just to forgive us our sins and to cleanse us from all unrighteousness." ~1 John 1:9 (NKJV)

If we have asked Jesus to forgive us, it's forgiven, it's forgotten, and it's time to do ourselves a favor and forgive ourselves.

What happens, though, when others won't allow us to move on? What do we do when those around us continue to mention things we did in the past or things we did that hurt someone else?

Everything we've worked on up to this point can be used here as well. With healing comes a new life entirely. It also comes with a forgiveness that makes us whole again. We are no longer who we used to be, so we have no business going back to what we used to do. We have no business going where we used to go.

It's very difficult sometimes to move forward when someone is blocking our way. This is what the enemy likes to do. He will attack our mind with vicious thoughts, or even use another person to come along and verbally attack us, using things from our past.

With that in mind, we have to focus on what's ahead of us and be mindful of where we are going. We all have a goal to meet. Having said that, let's look at how the Apostle Paul handled moving toward his goal.

Read Philippians 3:13-14
What did Paul focus on? _____
_____

Instead of looking back, what did he do? _____
_____

Now read verse 16. What must we hold on to? _____

When we walk healed we will not only have a new life, we will also run into struggles. Many of these will be with people who don't want to forgive. Some of these issues will even be within ourselves in the form of struggling to forgive ourselves. But we must not look backward. We must "press on" as Paul says in Philippians, looking toward the goal, which is our eternity in heaven with Jesus.

As we journey, God gives us various little divine appointments to share what He has done in our lives with those around us. If we're constantly looking back, how can we extend forgiveness and show others how to forgive?

Look at Colossians 3:13 (NLT) below.

"Make allowance for each other's faults, and forgive anyone who offends you. Remember, the Lord forgave you, so you must forgive others."

Who are we supposed to forgive? _____

We are to make allowance for each other's faults. This does not mean that we are to make excuses for them, just allowances. Okay, they messed up. We forgive them. Don't you think that could also be applied to yourself? Okay, you messed up. Forgive yourself.

We've looked at many passages throughout the section of forgiving others and forgiving ourselves. When it comes right down to it, every one of them can apply to both. The truth of the matter is this: Jesus forgave all of us. When we learn to accept that in both directions, we can move forward with the abundant life He died to give us.

God wants to show us so much more than we can even realize, if we'll just release ourselves from our self-appointed condemnation and embrace the forgiveness that has been ours the entire time we've been wasting time.

Jeremiah 33:3 states, "Call to Me and I will answer you and show you great and mighty things which you do not know." (NKJV)

I want to know those great and mighty things, don't you?

SECTION THREE: GRACE - EXTENDING GRACE AND RECEIVING GRACE

"For the Lord God is a sun and a shield; The Lord will give grace and glory; No good thing will He withhold from those who walk uprightly." ~Psalm 84:11 (NKJV)

When we find forgiveness for ourselves and others, we will also find grace. Not to be confused with mercy, grace has a similar meaning, but is entirely different. Let's look at them before we move on.

Mercy – God NOT punishing us as our sins deserve.

Grace – God BLESSING us despite the fact we don't deserve it.

Mercy – Not receiving the punishment we deserve.

Grace – Receiving blessings we don't deserve.

Keep these definitions in mind as we go through the next few lessons. We are going to start with extending grace to others.

Extending Grace (Giving Grace to Others)

Many people who have been hurt or abused by others want to hold on to what happened and continually hang on to that hurt, mistrust, anger, bitterness, and all those other feelings we harbor. It's the way we've always been—and in our mind we justify our pain without any work to improve.

Once we've accepted forgiveness we are able to give grace—that blessing that's undeserved, yet God gives it and so should we.

Grace works in conjunction with forgiveness. We want to hold a grudge, but we let it go instead. That's grace. We want to be bitter, but we embrace peace and choose to be better. That's grace.

It doesn't mean that we go back into a relationship with those who have abused or hurt us. We can reconcile, but we don't go back to the same level we once were at with that person. Grace doesn't mean we go back. Grace propels us forward and onward.

Moving Forward (pg. 74)

We've talked about healing. We've talked about forgiveness. So now what do we do? After the healing, after we learn how to forgive others and ourselves, what's next? It's time to move forward. It's time to walk healed.

God healed you for a reason. He has a plan for you and it's a big one. You may not realize it or even know what that is yet, and we'll talk more about finding your purpose in the last section of this study. But for now, we need to take it one step at a time and move toward that in learning how to extend grace not only to others, but also for ourselves as well.

When God heals you of an issue, or even several issues that you kept buried deep within, you will come out of it into a new light. When the newness wears off, that's when moving forward really begins. By staying in prayer, reading your Bible, you will stay grounded in Him.

We have to move forward in our journey if we are to be successful and grow in our spiritual walk. We cannot afford to stay where we are. We simply can't stay here. It's very important to move forward. And yes, there will be those who try to keep us from going forth. But let me give you some encouragement straight from God's Word.

"Devote yourselves to prayer; stay alert in it with thanksgiving." ~Colossians 4:2 (HCSB)

In your own words, what does it mean to "devote yourselves to prayer?"

_____
_____
_____

We need to make a commitment to talk to the Lord every single day. We also need to pay attention (stay alert) and also be thankful.

Look at Colossians 4:5-6 (NLT) below.

"Live wisely among those who are not believers, and make the most of every opportunity. Let your conversation be gracious and attractive so that you will have the right response for everyone."

It's not enough to *just* talk to the Lord every day and read our Bibles. There's so much more to this journey than that. Every day we come in contact with unbelievers. Whether we realize it or not, they are constantly watching us.

How are we to live among those who are not believers? _____

What are we to do with every opportunity? _____

How are we to handle our conversations and why? _____
_____

Growing up, I hated to be grounded. It meant that I was confined and couldn't go anywhere or talk to anyone. But with God, being grounded isn't like that. When God heals us (grace), He helps us move forward (more grace), so we can help others (even more grace.) Only when we are grounded will we be able to move forward and be able to extend and receive grace.

Grace Who? (pg. 104)

When we talk about grace, sometimes it may be easy to think of grace as a "who" and not a "what." When we meet Jesus, we begin to understand grace. Or at least, we should. Remember, grace is receiving blessings we don't deserve. God blessing us despite the fact we don't deserve it. Some of us take a little longer to figure out grace than others.

How can we better understand grace? Let's look at a definition from dictionary.com: ***"favor or goodwill, manifestation of goodwill, kindness, mercy, clemency, pardon."***
Now look at Psalm 84:11 below from the NKJV.

"For the Lord God is a sun and shield; The Lord will give grace and glory; No good thing will He withhold from those who walk uprightly."

Compare the two for just a moment. What do you notice about a secular definition of grace and a spiritual one? If you'll notice in the dictionary definition it talks about favor or goodwill. In the Scripture it clearly states that the Lord "will give grace and glory" and "No good thing will He withhold" from those of us who walk uprightly. There's the favor He shows us. That is grace.

Let's look at another passage.

"But He gives more grace. Therefore He says: "God resists the proud, But give grace to the humble." ~James 4:6 (NKJV)

He gives *more* grace?

To whom does He give more grace to? _____
Who does it say God resists? _____

If God can give more grace to those who humble themselves and choose to follow Him and do what His Word says, wouldn't it be in our best interest to give more grace to those around us as well? What if we were to forgive those who have hurt us, then extend grace to them by showing clemency, pardon, and kindness?

It doesn't necessarily mean that we rekindle a relationship, though if we were to be able to do that it would be a big step. You may be able to do that with some, yet with others you cannot. Some of those people may still be around, some may not be.

If Jesus loved us enough to give us His forgiveness, grace, and mercy, we should also do as He did.

Comfort Training (111)

"[God] comforts us in all our troubles so that we can comfort others. When they are troubled, we will be able to give them the same comfort God has given us." ~2 Corinthians 1:4 (NLT)

We may not realize it when we are going through certain issues, but God may be going to use those things we go through as a sort of training so that we will be able to extend grace to others who are suffering the things God healed us from.

Maybe that sounds like a lot right now, but think about it. Comfort training.

Look back at the above Scripture.

Which troubles does God comfort us through? _____

What reason does it give that He does this? _____

When others are troubled, what will we be able to do? _____

_____

Why do you suppose that was repeated? Could it be that God thought it was important enough for us to remember? All the things we go through at the time, we often think we're the only ones going through it. Yet later on, we may discover someone who is going through what we once did. We may remember how God brought us through it. That's when we will be able to comfort someone else "with the same comfort God has given us."

It's ironic that the lives of some people have paralleled ours. That's how life is. That's how God works. He takes each of us on a journey. He gives each of us a story to tell. He comforts us so we can comfort others in the same way. Why?

Read the passage below then write your answer to the above question in the space provided.

"...And you will be my witnesses in Jerusalem, and in all Judea and Samaria, and to the ends of the earth." ~Acts 1:8(b) (NIV)

_____
_____
_____

Through all the years I suffered depression, anxiety, intimidation, and the mental and emotional abuse from others, God was training me to comfort others. He was training me to testify to others what He has done for me.

Never underestimate God or how far He will go to reach someone.

Let me insert a small disclaimer in this section before we go any further. Please understand that the things we go through, the hurts, sickness, depression, abuse, whatever those things are that we have no control over yet happen to us anyway, these things God is not causing to happen. God doesn't want to afflict us. Yet, He often allows us to go through trials in order to reach us and teach us, thereby equipping us to better serve Him and also to help bring others into healing and a better relationship with Him.

Look at James 1:2-3 from the NLT.

"Dear brothers and sisters, when troubles come your way, consider it an opportunity for great joy. For you know that when your faith is tested, your endurance has a chance to grow."

It may be hard to find joy in our afflictions or trials. They turn out to be an opportunity to increase our faith in the Lord.

However, we must also remember that our great enemy, the devil, is also prowling and watching, always looking for someone he can devour and destroy (1 Peter 5:8). But take a look at what the next verse says and be encouraged.

"Resist him, steadfast in the faith, knowing that the same sufferings are experienced by your brotherhood in the world." ~1 Peter 5:9 (NKJV)

Knowing that our brothers and sisters in Christ all over the world are also going through trials and experiences can help us get through tough situations. We know that the enemy is attacking all of us. But we also know that God loves us and will come to our rescue when we call to Him

So why do people still ask, "Where was God when this happened to me?" That could have many different answers. But regardless, our faith in Him should only increase. He gives us grace to get through everything. Look at the verse below.

"And He said to me, "My grace is sufficient for you, for My strength is made perfect in weakness..." ~2 Corinthians 12:9(a) (NKJV)

It all comes back to grace. His grace. His grace is sufficient, enough, for us. And in our weaknesses, when we're going through trials and things that we wish we weren't, or that we can't figure out how to get out of or why God isn't getting us out of them, we need to remember His grace is enough. That in itself should be enough to give us peace, knowing it will soon be over and we will come out of it victorious and can then move on with a testimony that will help someone else.

My Chains Are Gone! (pg. 137)

In this chapter, it begins with a quote from a man who spoke these words as encouragement for someone who was going through a bit of testing after being set free.

"Your chains are broken and you truly are free. So shake off your chains and move forward!"

How ironic that everything that has been said in this workbook has pointed to being free and moving forward, yet before the writing of this book, a very Godly man spoke them as he was led by the Holy Spirit, to reach someone in need. Me. And now, you.

The enemy knows that when we go boldly to the throne of grace, amazing things happen.

Read the verse below then write what really happens when the Son (Jesus) makes us free.

"So if the Son liberates you [makes you free men], then you are really and unquestionably free." ~John 8:36 (Amplified Bible)

_____
_____

If we really are free, why then do we question it when the above verse says we are "unquestionably free?" Because the enemy of our souls wants to keep us in fear and frustration so that we don't move forward. He wants to keep us in bondage so that we don't live free.

But once our chains are broken, they can't be put back together and put back on us.

Sometimes the enemy likes to sidetrack us. It may not seem like an enemy attack. It may seem like a friend has turned her back on us. It may seem like a family member has shunned us. It's hurtful.

Remember, Jesus went through the same things. He understands. We need to remember that He has also provided a safe place to run to: Him.

Read the verses below, then write every way the Lord is a protection to us.

"The name of the Lord is a strong tower; the [consistently] righteous man [upright and in right standing with God] runs into it and is safe, high [above evil] and strong." **~Proverbs 18:10 (Amplified Bible)**

"For You have been a shelter and a refuge for me, a strong tower against the adversary." **~Psalm 61:3 (Amplified Bible)**

_____
_____

Who or what does the Lord protect us from? _____

How are we instructed to come to Him? How does it say the righteous come? _____
_____

When we come to the Lord, we should run. We should come boldly and we should come without fear, and with confidence because He is for us and not against us. The enemy is against us, remember that. God is not against us.

When our chains are broken, everything changes. We need to watch and listen. Be ready for God to do something amazing and wonderful. Because of His grace, He will instill in you the same power to give grace to those around you.

Part Two - Receiving Grace

Because I Love You (pg. 164)

Sometimes we waste too much time. We waste it in fear, whether it's fear of what might happen or fear of what others may say. However, when we have lived in depression, anxiety, intimidation, or whatever circumstance God has healed us from, we can begin to understand how that has affected those around us as well. In our wounded world we often wound the ones closest to us and not even know it. It was that way with my husband and me.

As a wounded soul, we take those who actually love and support us with no strings attached and we slide them into the same role as the people who hurt us for many years. We see everyone as a potential to hurt us, so we handle them always defensively, even if they never do anything to cause us pain. We often don't realize that in doing so, we are also causing more hurt to those who would never hurt us.

We have to get to a place where we know what is causing our continual fear, anxiety, depression and intimidation. We have to get our priorities going the right direction and realize who we are in order to be able to extend and receive grace.

Look at the passage below and write who it says we are.

"For we are God's masterpiece. He has created us anew in Christ Jesus, so we can do the good things he planned for us long ago." ~Ephesians 2:10 (NLT)

Who are we? _____

How are we created? _____

What are we created for? _____

_____

When did He plan this for us? _____

God did all of this because He loves us. "Because I love you," would probably be the words He would say if you asked Him why. That is grace.

Look at those around you. With me, it was my husband. When questioned why he was still with me after nearly thirty years of dealing with my depression, anxiety, and intimidation, he only had one answer, "Because I love you." My husband loved me enough to stay with me, showing me the love of Jesus, and help me. God loves me enough to help me. He loves you enough to help you, too.

Look at Ephesians 2:4-8 (NLT). Read along in your Bible (or Bible app) to find the words and fill in the blanks.

"But God is so rich in _____, and he loved us so much, that even though we were dead because of our sins, he gave us life when he raised Christ from the dead. (It is only by God's _____ that you have been saved!) For he raised us from the dead along with Christ and seated us with him in the heavenly realms because we are united with Christ Jesus. So God can point to us in all future ages and examples of the incredible wealth of his _____ and kindness toward us, as shown in all he has done for us who are untied with Christ.

God saved you by his _____ when you believed. And you can't take credit for this; it is a gift from God."

Because of God's mercy and grace, we are saved. Because of His love for us, He extends mercy and grace to us. When we receive healing from Him, we are able to extend and receive mercy and grace to others.

It's all out of love.

Don't Back Up (pg. 168)

When we are making progress in our lives, especially after God heals us and we are on the road He wants us on, it's important to know that we will experience someone or something that will come alongside us and try to knock us back down. It's important to know that we cannot back up.

Knowing my healing story, it's crucial in what I do now. It's even more important that I tell others. Without the healing I wouldn't be doing what I'm doing today. You wouldn't be doing this study, or reading my book. I can't back up. You can't back up, either.

"I don't mean to say that I have already achieved these things or that I have already reached perfection. But I press on to possess that perfection for which Christ Jesus first possessed me." ~Philippians 3:12 (NLT)

In the above verse, what is it that we should press on to do? _____
_____

None of us are perfect just yet. But we should all be moving forward to possess it as Christ first possessed us. In my case the statement, "You've come a long way, baby," is true. I have come a long way. If you've received Jesus as your Lord and Savior, if you've received healing, you've come a long way too, baby! Just don't back up.

We should all be a walking billboard for the Lord. It doesn't mean that we always "get it." Because frankly, most of the time I don't even get it. What I do get is that God has called me out and called me to a ministry of reaching others who are in the same pit I once was in.

Look at the following verse.

"No, dear brothers and sisters, I have not achieved it, but I focus on this one thing: Forgetting the past and looking forward to what lies ahead..." ~Philippians 3:13(a) (NLT)

What does it tell us we should focus on? _____

Where should we be looking? _____

When we focus on forgetting what's in the past and focus on looking forward to what lies ahead, we will be well on our way in our journey. It's not about what we're going through. It's about where our focus lies.

Where should we put our focus, 100%? _____ (pg. 169)

If you look at Hebrews 12:1b-2a, it says that we are to *"run with endurance the race that is set before us."* We are all in a race, but not with each other. This race is individual. It's personal. And the only way we can get through it is by *"looking unto Jesus, the author and finisher of our faith."*

If you have backed up, how do you expect God to help you? He's waiting ahead of you for you to catch up. Yes, we will have trials. We will have seasons when it seems easier for us to back up. However, even though we do, if we will move forward God in His infinite grace will be there.

Isaiah 43:2-3(a) (NLT) is the epitome of grace. Write it below in your own words.

_____
_____
_____
_____
_____
_____

Even when we go through deep waters, rivers of difficulty, and the fires of oppression, what does God promise? _____

No matter what we go through God, the LORD, the Holy One of Israel, our Savior, promises that He will be with us. That, dear lovelies, is grace. Whatever you do, don't back up!

What Are You Doing Here? (pg. 181)

Being intimidated by other people doesn't mean that you're afraid. It doesn't mean you don't want to come out in the open. I was the same way. Though it would be very easy to become agoraphobic (someone who is so afraid she never leaves her home), sometimes it seems as if it would just be easier to stay within those four walls.

The prophet Elijah went through some of the same things. He became afraid and ran away.

But look what happened in 1 Kings 19:3(a), 9 (NLT):
"Elijah was afraid and fled for his life... There he came to a cave, where he spent the night. But the LORD said to him, "What are you doing here, Elijah?"

Elijah's moment of fear came on the heels of a great victory. He had killed all the prophets of a false god and someone told on him. Imagine that. Therefore, someone else wanted to kill him for it. So Elijah got scared and ran.

But here's where grace stepped in: even though Elijah ran, God still took care of him.

What was the question God asked Elijah? _____

Maybe we think we can't handle the confrontations of others or their attacks, or even the attack of the enemy (which by the way comes in the form of the above mentioned things), so we decide to run. Hole up in our house, in the darkness of our room, or maybe run to another state, another country, or find some remote place where no one else can find us. But guess Who is already there waiting? God.

Is there anywhere we can go that God isn't? Is there anywhere we can hide that He won't find us?

Read the passage below then answer that question in the space provided.

"O LORD, you have examined my heart and know everything about me...I can never escape from your Spirit! I can never get away from your presence!" ~Psalm 139:1, 7 (NLT)

Where can we go that God won't be there? _____

God is everywhere, all the time. There is nowhere that we can go where He can't or won't find us. In truth, there is nowhere we can go that God is not already there. If you read all of Psalm 139, you will see that God knows everything about you, inside and out.

People may threaten us, ridicule us, embarrass, bully, intimidate, oppress, or verbally and mentally abuse us. But we don't have to run like Elijah did. It may be a difficult thing to do, but we can smile and show them grace, just as God shows us.

Be confident today that no matter what anyone does, trying to attack us, they will not succeed.

Read Isaiah 54:17. What is the promise in that passage?
_____
_____

God is always on your side, lovely one. You have too much to do to allow someone to keep you in hiding. What are you doing here? Get out there and go back the way you came. Stand tall. Stand confident.

Where Do I Go From Here? (pg. 209)

So, what happens after the healing? What happens after we learn to forgive others and then forgive ourselves? What happens when we learn to receive grace and also extend it to others? What then? Where *do* we go from here?

Life isn't perfect. I won't lie about that. We will still have trials, moments of frustration, and people who will want to shut us up. There will still be people who try to intimidate, oppress, threaten, ridicule, and try to convince others that you're not what or who you say you are. I find this very sad.

The question you may be asking right now is, "How do I determine whether or not negative, or confrontational people should have my personal attention?" We looked at three things to consider when someone is trying to give advice or tell you what they think you should do.

Look back at pages 210 and 211 in Walking Healed. What were those three things?

1. _____
2. _____
3. _____

Some people may say that to separate yourself from people who cause you problems is being petty. Let's address this now.

Look at Romans 16:17 (NKJV) below. What does it say we are to do?
"Now I urge you, brethren, note those who cause divisions and offenses, contrary to the doctrine which you learned, and avoid them."

_____
_____
_____

There will be those who want to convince you that they are Christians, but act totally opposite. These are they who feel threatened by what you are embarking on. Why? Because they are not following the path God laid out for them. They are under conviction by the Holy Spirit. Instead of doing what the Lord is calling them to do, they lash out at ones who are following their calling.

What does 1 Corinthians 5:11 say we are to do with those who call themselves brothers (Christians) yet act the total opposite? _____
_____

This doesn't mean that we are to totally shun them. Remember what Jesus said in **Matthew 18:21-22** about forgiveness. We are to forgive. But by keeping our distance from those who say they're a Christian yet don't act according to what the Bible says, we are also showing grace. Love them, just keep your distance.

A great way to show forgiveness and grace to those who would try to attack us is by first praying for them. Then, move on and not dwell on things that try to get us down. Remember, the three things above when others try to drag us into drama and intimidation:

Is it positive?

Is it helpful?

Is it godly?

Seek the advice of the Holy Spirit above all and when you do, everything will begin to take shape.

I hope that you have discovered by now that healing, forgiveness, and grace are all tied together. You can't have one without the other. When we are healed we begin to forgive, not only others but ourselves. When we begin to forgive, we receive and are able to extend grace.

Grace doesn't mean we go back. We don't go back into toxic relationships, friendships, or activities. Grace propels us forward. We move ahead into relationships, friendships and activities that fortify us and help us work and move into the life and plan God has for us.

We don't try to destroy others because of their sins—instead, grace extends forgiveness and moves on. How do we extend grace though, when we don't want to?

We need to look at a few things. Go back to the beginning of our lessons and re-evaluate:

Where do our feelings of distrust, anxiety, anger, dislike (hatred), stem from?

Are these issues you need to confront or confess?

If you still harbor these things or carry them in your heart, mind, or spirit, then you haven't forgiven or let them go.

Go back to Healing:

Have you received healing from the Lord?

Yes? Move on to Forgiveness.

Have you forgiven? Others? Yourself?

Remember: You have to forgive in order to be forgiven.

Look at Matthew 6:15 (NKJV) below.

"But if you do not forgive men their trespasses, neither will your Father forgive your trespasses."

If we don't forgive others, what does it is say about our Father (God)? _____
_____

Once you receive healing and accept and extend forgiveness, you can give grace. Once you forgive, don't pick it back up. When you give grace you don't continue to bring up the wrong, or try to make that person pay for their mistake again, and again. You can't say, "I forgive you," then down the road, remind that person of their offense.

Look back at the beginning of this section and write the definition of Grace below (remember, grace and mercy have similar meanings, but are very different).
_____
_____
_____

It doesn't matter what's in the past. We need to find and extend forgiveness and grace and then move on with our lives. Leave it alone. Don't go back—move forward. When we do that, we'll begin to find hope.

A Time of Prayer

Think of a way you can extend grace today. Choose a Scripture from the lessons or a memory verse and write a prayer of grace in the space provided. Let it come from your heart.

SECTION FOUR: HOPE

"And now, Lord, what do I wait for and expect? My hope and expectation are in You."

~Psalm 39:7 (Amplified Bible)

We have talked about a lot of things throughout this study. We've talked about healing, which is the first and biggest step to walking healed. Having a relationship with Jesus (salvation) is top priority. We've learned that even as Christians, we can still suffer depression, addiction, abuse, intimidation, etc., which all keep us from walking healed and free. We've also talked about being able to forgive (others and ourselves) once we're healed. How much easier it is to forgive when we're free from the burdens of un-forgiveness.

We've talked about extending grace (undeserved blessings) to others and ourselves. When we show grace, we need to move on. Don't back up or continue in unhealthy relationships or activities.

So now what? I have addressed you throughout this study as "dear lovelies," and "lovely ones." It may seem a bit forward, because, honestly lovelies, we may have never met before. However, even though I may not have seen your beautiful face, I know that you're beautiful. I know you're a lovely one. I know this because you were created by the same hands that created me. We are kindred spirits, dearest. We have the same heavenly Father. Because we are joint heirs with Jesus, we are also of the same spiritual family, so that makes us siblings in Christ.

That may seem like a lot to process, but having gone through the previous lessons in healing, forgiveness and grace, knowing that you are beautiful because God made you and that we are all spiritually related, brings us to our next section: Hope.

What is hope?

According to Siri on my iPhone, the definition of hope is ***"A feeling of expectation and desire for a certain thing to happen. A feeling of trust."***

Hope is *Jesus*. Hope is the anticipation of "my life is getting better." Hope is moving to the next level, *trusting* the Lord and at the same time knowing that no matter what, you are healed and God's got you safely in His hands; *anticipating* that He is there to help you at all times.

That is hope.

When you allow God to do something big in you—in my case it was healing me of over forty years of emotional garbage, intimidation and abuse—He not only changes that but He turns your whole life upside-right! Yes, I said upside-right because nothing is ever upside-down anymore.

When God turns your life upside-right, He also begins to install new software into your hard drive. Everything begins to change, your attitude, your outlook, your thought process, even your feelings and actions.

I jokingly say I'm still learning what to do with my healed self. Yet, it's true and I'll continue learning every day. You will too. That in itself should give you hope of something wonderful and exciting to come. You should look forward to it.

Every day the Bible says God gives us something new. Clarity of mind, sharpness inside, new faith, spiritual gifts and awareness, ability to forgive, ability to move forward and move on, speak to people, help others, whatever you have been called to do He is there to help you every day to carry those things out as only you can do.

Hope is when I look forward to what's next with no fear because I know He has great big plans for me.

Read Jeremiah 29:11-13 from the NLT. What kind of plans does God have for us?
_____

What does He say He will do when we pray? _____

If we look for God, in what way are we to look? What does that mean to you?
_____
_____
_____

When we search for Him seriously, wholeheartedly, with all our hearts, what does He promise? _____

God's plan for us is perfect because He is perfect. There is no way you can mess up His plan for you, no matter what you've been through or done. Someone once said that God's Plan A trumps your Plan B any day. Perfectly.

Perfectly, Powerfully, and Permanently (pg. 120)

God loves you perfectly, powerfully, and permanently. Period. He will never turn His back on you. God doesn't get mad at you. He also promised He would never leave you (Hebrews 5). God's love in you produces the fruit of the Spirit, making us capable to love and receive love. Just like His healing causes a domino effect of sorts that when we are healed we find forgiveness. When we find forgiveness we find grace, and when we find grace are able to find hope.

Read Galatians 5:22-23 from the NLT below then write what each of the fruit in our lives are. _____
_____

"But the Holy Spirit produces this kind of fruit in our lives: love, joy, peace, patience, kindness, goodness, faithfulness, gentleness, and self-control. There is no law against these things!"

Who produces this fruit? _____

In God's infinite wisdom, when we accepted Jesus we were given these fruits. How they manifest in our lives is by reading God's Word, staying in communication with Him (prayer), and by living each day focused on Him. This is how our hope is increased. By staying as close to Him as possible.

Yes, we'll mess up. We aren't perfect. But because God forgives and forgets we can move on when we've confessed to Him. That all by itself is enough to give hope. Trust God, not your feelings. Feelings can be fickle. The enemy will twist and turn them to manipulate you into believing that you need people, places, money, etc. in order to be happy when all you really need is Jesus.

Moving On! (pg. 128)

It's one thing to write about, think about, or even talk about being healed, forgiving, or even showing grace. What you have to do to actually live it is move on from there. There is so much more to your journey than where you're at right now. So much has happened, but so much more awaits. There's more to learn and there's more to give. There is so much hope waiting for you.

There are people who are suffering who need to know that there is hope for them. What if you never stepped out of your own little box to share your story? It's time to move on. It's time to move up. Put your shoes on, dear lovelies and let God lead you into something wonderful. Don't know how? Read the verse below and see if it helps point you in the right direction.

"Jesus told him, "I am the way, the truth, and the life. No one can come to the Father except through me." ~ **John 14:6 (NLT)**

What three things did Jesus say He is? _____
How do we get to God the Father? _____

It may sound trivial, but unless you have a relationship with Jesus the healing doesn't happen, forgiveness doesn't happen, grace doesn't happen, and hope certainly doesn't add into the equation. Therefore, you can never move on or up. Only a relationship with Jesus can get you all of these and more.

But if you never move on from your past, your situation, your issues, or even from the wonderful things Jesus does for you in this instant, you can never help anyone else nor give others hope of being free from the same issues they suffer. You also won't live in hope of the wonderful things God can do for you along your journey.

That may sound redundant, but I can't stress it enough. There's an old hymn that many still sing today. The words to the chorus go, "I shall not be, I shall not be moved; I shall not be, I shall not be moved; Just like a tree that's planted by the waters, Lord, I shall not be moved." Many people sing that song and then they live it out literally in that they plant their roots and refuse to move even outside their comfort zone to even help another who needs to hear their healing story.

Can't Keep Me Down (pg. 131)

As we move on in our journey, of course we will have trials and there will be people who want to try to keep us down. But the exciting thing about this journey is that God won't allow you to be kept down any longer.

Look at the verse below then write what it is that depends on God.

"My defense and shield depend on God, Who saves the upright in heart." ~Psalm 7:10 (Amplified Bible)

_____

Who does God save? _____

You need to realize that Jesus was knocked down, too. He also got back up. Because of what He did on the cross, He made a way for you and me to be able to get back up when the chips are down.

No more do you have to be held down by ugly words, manipulative actions of others, or anything that seeks to destroy you. We can have hope that He will rescue us when these things happen. We can be confident that He is on our side. We can smile, knowing that when someone tries to put us down God won't let us be kept down.

Let's take a look at one more verse below.

"And now, Lord, what do I wait for and expect? My hope and expectation are in You." ~Psalm 39:7 (Amplified Bible)

Whom do we wait for? _____
Where is our hope and expectation? _____

If we wait for, expect, and our hope and expectation are all in the Lord, what really can anyone else do to keep us down? Absolutely nothing.

Where Do I Fit In? (pg. 133)

Where *do* I fit in? Many people today are asking this question. It starts in childhood, wanting to fit in with the other kids, a certain group, club, organization, and various other things throughout our lives. We run ourselves ragged trying to figure out where our niche is. What are we good at? What is our talent? What can we do that will allow us to fit in with others? But too often we are asking the wrong questions for the wrong reasons.

The answer to all these questions is we don't fit in with anything and anyone associated with this world. While we try so hard to get people to like us, to be accepted into one clique or club after another, we forget that we have fit in all along with God.

I think I heard a disappointed sigh or groan there. If so, let me encourage you with this: God loves you so very much. He created you. Therefore, *you* matter!

Want to find out how you matter? Read the passage below.

"For we are God's masterpiece. He has created us anew in Christ Jesus, so we can do the good things he planned for us long ago." ~Ephesians 2:10 (NLT)

What does this verse say we are? _____

Who created us? _____ *In whom?* _____

For what reason did He create us? _____

_____

When did he plan this? _____

God doesn't just create dull things. He creates a masterpiece every time He creates something or someone. So you, beautiful one, are no accident. You are something unique, special, and wonderful. You fit in with G-O-D Himself. He is interested in y-o-u.

Even though I wear mismatched socks and have purple hair, God loves me and I fit in just where He wants me to fit. Just like a puzzle piece, He has placed me where He wants me to reach those He wants me to reach. You are the same way. You are the way you are because there is someone God wants you to reach.

The next time you wonder where you fit in, ask God. Then be prepared to receive what He tells you and act on it.

Ch-Ch-Ch-Changes (pg. 145)

Although we change every day, nearly every minute, Jesus never does. My grandpa once told me, "Jesus is the only constant in this world." He was right. We like everything to stay the same, yet we are always changing our minds and really, when you think about it, we don't like change. We are our own oxymoron.

If we don't make changes we won't grow. It doesn't matter if it's physical, mental, emotional, or spiritual, change is often quite a good thing; especially if it helps you to move forward and into what God has prepared for you.

Let's take a look at Philippians 3:21 (NLT) and see what happens when we trust God for our changes.

"He will take our weak mortal bodies and change them into glorious bodies like his own, using the same power with which he will bring everything under his control."

What does God change our bodies into? _____
How does He do it? _____
What are your thoughts on this passage? _____
_____

God has the power to change our bodies in an instant. He will do that with everyone one day when Jesus comes back. However, until then, can He do it now? Can He actually take our bodies and make them whole again, heal us, restore us? Yes! He can. And He wants to. The question is, do you want Him to?

Part of the hope we live in and walk in is that God keeps His promises and will do what He says He will do. Healing His children is part of that. Yet, we often struggle with want versus need when it comes to God healing us, or forgiving us, or receiving grace, walking in hope, or even finding our purpose.

In my journey, my want became my need. But though I needed healing, I struggled with whether or not I wanted it. That would mean change. Would it hurt? Would it be worth it? Would my life take a different path? So many questions. So many answers I didn't have.

But I had hope. I had that hope that God would do what He promised, but He would also do what He needed to do to get me where He wanted me. And the time had come that He definitely had me where He wanted me. That's when He healed me.

Look at Lamentations 3:22-23 from the English Standard Version (ESV).

"The steadfast love of the LORD never ceases; his mercies never come to an end; they are new every morning; great is your faithfulness."

What does it say never ceases? _____

What never comes to an end? _____

    What hope is in that the Lord's love, His steadfast love, never ceases. That means it never stops. It is strong enough and abundant enough that it never stops for us. Included in that, His mercies never come to an end. Never.

But look at the last part of that verse again.
What is new and when is it? _____

    If His mercies are new every morning that must mean that they are different from the day before. Changes. We get new stuff every day from a never-changing God. So, if yesterday I *wanted* healing but today I *need* it, will He supply it? You bet He will.

Rejoice in the following verse:
"And this same God who takes care of me will supply all your needs from his glorious riches, which have been given to us in Christ Jesus." ~Philippians 4:19 (NLT)

    Yes, lovelies, our needs change every day. But our "same God" takes care of us supplies all our needs from his glorious riches.

    That right there is enough to place my hope in.

I Am a Lazarus (pg. 155)

Are you a Lazarus? I am. I am a walking, talking miracle. Unlike the real Lazarus, whom Jesus raised from the dead, I wasn't physically dead. Nor was I spiritually dead because I had accepted Jesus in salvation a little over thirty years earlier. I was nearly emotionally dead though, from over forty years of depression, anxiety, intimidation, and mental garbage that I had suffered. These things had nearly caused me permanent destruction and I was on the verge of never coming out of the pit I had been pressed down into for so long. That is, until Jesus called me out of it like He did Lazarus.

I'm sure Lazarus' sisters, Mary and Martha, felt quite hopeless when they sent for Jesus and He didn't get there in time before their brother died.

But look at what Jesus said in John 11:4 from the Holman Christian Standard Bible. It changes everything.

"When Jesus heard it, He said, "This sickness will not end in death but is for the glory of God, so that the Son of God may be glorified through it."

It may seem as if the things you're going through won't ever end, or that they'll end badly. But what does the above verse say Lazarus' sickness was for?

_____

Everything we go through is a potential to show the glory of God and to give Him glory. It may seem differently to you, especially when you're smack in the middle of troubles.

What does it say in John 11:25-26? _____

_____

What did Jesus say about everyone who believes in Him?

_____

_____

When we choose to believe Jesus over the lies of the enemy or those the enemy entices to attack us, amazing and miraculous things happen. We become a walking talking miracle, just like Lazarus.

Rose-Colored Glasses (pg. 174)

It's easy to look at the world through rose-colored glasses. To see things so distorted that you don't know what's the truth and what isn't. Being healed does not mean that things are always bright and cheery, either. There will still be people who try to intimidate us. But we don't have to allow it.

Having hope means that we are looking always at Jesus, waiting for Him, serving Him, and knowing that He is on my side and He's working everything out for my good. So how do we handle it when the negative things come our way?

Read Ephesians 6:14 (NLT) below:
"Stand your ground, putting on the belt of truth and the body armor of God's righteousness."

What are the first three words in that passage? _____ _____ _____
What are we to put on? _____

It may seem like God is quiet during times when people are jabbing us with all kinds of drama and negativity. Some like to confront us in person, others with a phone call. Regardless, we must stand our ground. The enemy uses many people to control and intimidate us. Sadly, some people don't even realize they're doing it. So how can we prevent ourselves from becoming victims again?

Read James 4:7-8(a). What is the first thing we are to do? _____
When we resist the devil what does he do? _____
What happens when we come close to God? _____

If God is close to us, how can the devil possibly stick around? Then again, if God is close to us, how could anyone possibly try to negatively influence us? I don't believe they can.

People may think you walk around with rose-colored glasses on because of your relationship with the Lord. Let them.

In the chapter Rose-Colored Glasses, there are nine things mentioned that have happened because of healing. (pg. 176) Write them on the lines provided on the next page.

_____
_____
_____

If Jesus sets you free, what does John 8:36 tell you that you are?

_____

God's Favor…is NOW! (pg. 191)

God wants you to know that His favor is now. His favor means approval, blessing, increase. In this chapter it mentions that God is raising up an army of women. Now. There are too many women who are being used, abused, and thrown aside like trash. But here's hope; God's favor is upon several women who have been rescued, healed, or brought out of some form of ill treatment in order to bring hope to others.

Read Luke 4:18-19
The Spirit of the Lord is on you. What has He anointed you to do? _____
_____

What is the last thing mentioned that has come? _____

What was the first thing I said in this chapter? God's favor is now. It's *now*, lovelies. We don't have to wait for it. He is dishing it out right now. No one will be left out, unless of course they choose not to receive it.

Let's look at some exciting hope that God dishes out for us by reading Romans 5:5 from the NLT.

"And this hope will not lead to disappointment. For we know how dearly God loves us, because he has given us the Holy Spirit to fill our hearts with his love."

Hope does not disappoint. We have favor with God because of His love for us and Jesus' sacrifice. God has something special just for you. You find your special something when you trust Him enough for healing, forgiveness, grace, and then the hope of what you already know in your heart, which comes directly from Him.

Read Hebrews 11:1. What goes along with hope? _____
What is it the evidence of? _____

Our hope comes from the faith we put in Jesus to carry out the promises that He made in His Word. When we place His word in our hearts, He begins to pour out His favor on us.

You have something special to offer to other girls and women, to give them encouragement and hope that there is something better out there. Don't be a victim any longer. God's favor is now. He's waiting for you with open arms.

Far Out! (pg. 194)

When God healed me, He gave me a promise, too. I was told that I would minister to women and give them encouragement and hope. Luke 4:18-19 became my signature verse because the Holy Spirit did come upon me the night I was healed and began to verify the promise (prophecy) that was spoken over me. It has grown since then and here we are today.

God never breaks His promises. If He told you something, it will happen.

In this chapter it mentions that hurting people hurt other people. What does it say about healed people? (pg. 195) _____

_____

You may be someone else's hope—they may see you and begin to wish (or hope) to have that excitement that you do. They may see that "you've got it all together," or have a "can do" mentality, or that "aura" or "something about you that's different." You know what it is and you get to show them what Jesus did for you. You may even get to introduce them to the Holy Spirit.

Walking healed is a combination of all the things we have talked about throughout these weeks of healing, forgiveness, grace, and now hope. How far out is that!

Look at one more passage before we move on. In Hebrews 6:19 it tells us what hope has become for us. Write it here. _____
What kind of anchor is hope for our souls? _____
Where does it lead us? _____
_____

If hope is a strong and trustworthy anchor that leads us through the curtain into God's inner sanctuary, then lovelies there isn't anything or anyone that can touch us. No matter what your storm is, God is the calm. If we put our trust and our hope in Him we will be anchored. To me, that's the most far out of all.

Discovering My More (pg. 200)

All too often we don't live up to our full potential. I was in a writing workshop at the home of author and speaker Patsy Clairmont a few years ago and she said these profound words: *"You are more than you know, and God is much more than you know. And people are more than we allow them to be."*

How true. In our finite minds we fail to live up to our more and even more miserably fail to allow others to be the more that they are. But the saddest thing is that we fail to see God in His so much more.

Look at Jeremiah 32:27 (NKJV). Write in the space below what is too hard for God.
"Behold, I am the LORD, the God of all flesh. Is there anything too hard for Me?"

_____

Hopefully you didn't write anything on that line.

If God is calling you to do something and you know it, step out in faith in Him and go for it. Because if God is calling you out, you can know right now that He will equip you to succeed. He wouldn't have called you if He didn't think He could get you through it, nor if He didn't think you could do it.

It's okay to ask Him how this will work, as long as you don't question His authority or His power. He will be happy to answer and show you exactly how if you are willing to allow Him to teach you.

When the angel visited Mary and told her she would conceive and bear a son, her reaction was not, "Are you crazy? I'm a virgin!" No, instead she asked how that could happen since she *was* a virgin.

Read Luke 1:34-36 for their conversation.

Now read Luke 1:37. What was the last thing the angel said to Mary?

_____

Mary was ready to discover her more. Are you? With nothing that is too hard for God, do you really think the plans He has for you are hard either?

The only way you're going to discover your more is by stepping out in faith and asking God to show you.

Changing Your Life (pg. 205)

People with anxiety and depression suffer. They also cause those around them to suffer as well. They may not mean to. They may not even realize they're doing it.

God did not give any of us depression, anxiety, or any other emotional or mental disorder. Yet, sometimes He does allow us to go through these things so that He can use them to move us forward and into the calling He has for our lives.

Read Psalm 138:8 and write it below.

_____
_____
_____
_____
_____

Knowing that the Lord works out His plans for our lives puts things in a new perspective, doesn't it? This is just confirmation that you are not hopeless nor are you a mistake.

You can break the cycle of generational curses. You can break the chains. You can change your life by changing how you speak over yourself and the lives of your children and children's children.

We may have family, friends, or even people we work with who speak negative over us, but we do have the power to change that. We can be healed. Don't let your history destroy your destiny. History is in the past. Destiny is in the future, it's forward and the only way to get there is to move on.

Look at Psalm 57:2-3 from the NLT.

"I cry out to God Most High, to God who will fulfill his purpose for me. He will send help from heaven to rescue me, disgracing those who hound me. My God will send forth his unfailing love and faithfulness."

What does God fulfill? _____

Where does He send help from? _____

What else does He send to us? _____

What happens to those who constantly cause us trouble? _____

God has our best interest at hand. Though we may go through a lot of trouble and strife, God has a purpose for it all. He doesn't leave us out in the cold to fend for ourselves. We have the power to change our lives and when we realize all we have to do is cry out to Him, He sends help straight from heaven to rescue us. This is how we maintain our hope. Knowing our Heavenly Father is there for us always.

Walking healed is so much more than healing, forgiveness, grace, and hope. It's an everyday activity. Choose to walk healed. Live on purpose because you *are* on purpose. You may be thinking, but what *is* my purpose? We're going to discuss that in our final section.

One More Thing

Earlier in this section we talked about hope being an anchor for our soul (Hebrews 6:19). But let's dig a bit deeper into that before we leave. If we take a look at the two verses before this we will learn something very great about our wonderful heavenly Father.

Read Hebrews 6:17-18 (NIV) below.
"Because God wanted to make the unchanging nature of his purpose very clear to the heirs of what was promised, he confirmed it with an oath. God did this so that, by two unchangeable things in which it is impossible for God to lie, we who have fled to take hold of the hope set before us may be greatly encouraged."
What two things did God make very clear in these two verses? _____
_____

First of all, God never changes. We can rest assured that no matter what happens in our lives, God remains the same always. Second, God cannot lie. He will never lie to you. Therefore, if something doesn't seem right to you where God is concerned then He's probably not in it.

God made sure that you had this in writing, in the Bible, so that you could look back on it whenever you needed encouragement. He thought this was important enough for you to know. That by itself should give you hope to move forward.

God never changes His mind or goes back on His word. He is trustworthy in all His promises and faithful in everything He does.

Let's look at Numbers 23:19 NIV

"God is not human, that he should lie, not a human being, that he should change his mind. Does he speak and then not act? Does he promise and not fulfill?
Now read the last part of Psalm 145:13 NIV

"...The LORD is trustworthy in all he promises and faithful in all he does."

Does God lie? _____
What two things does Psalm 145:13 prove? _____
_____

We can see the proof that God never changes, does not lie, and is faithful in everything He promises. He never backs out on His word. People will let us down, this is true. But God never will. We can walk in hope every day knowing that God has us in the palm of His hand, He has our back, and He will never let us down.

If you have trusted Jesus with your salvation, allowed Him to heal you, and are walking in that today you are a miracle, a masterpiece, and you have so much potential. You can now step out and walk in your purpose, knowing you are equipped by the Most High God to do wonderful things, lovely one.

Below is your chance to pray about your hope. Take a few minutes to think about that, then follow the instructions.

A Time of Prayer

Choose a Scripture from the lessons or a memory verse, then listen to your heart and write a prayer of hope in the space provided.

SECTION FIVE: FINDING YOUR PURPOSE

"But forget all that – it is nothing compared to what I am going to do. For I am about to do something new. See, I have already begun! Do you not see it? I will make a pathway through the wilderness. I will create rivers in the dry wasteland."
~Isaiah 43:18-19 (NLT)

We've come such a long way in our journey, lovely ones. From healing, to finding forgiveness, then extending grace, and on to living in hope, now we must continue our journey by finding our purpose. When we find our purpose we can inspire and encourage others, even help them find theirs. We are all connected by a holy cord known as the Holy Spirit. He's not a cord in the sense that He's a rope that ties us all together, but He is the person, the Spirit of Jesus, the Holy Spirit, our Helper, our Guide. He knows the will of the Father, He listens to Him, He intercedes for us, and then He helps us on our journey.

In this section we will discuss ways to discover our purpose. When we use the gifts and talents that God gives us, we are ultimately walking in our anointing and our calling (our purpose). When we go our own way, not doing what we feel God is wanting us to do, we are out of His will and therefore are not walking in our purpose. Being out of God's will is being in disobedience.

Sometimes we think it's one thing, but things just don't seem to be going the way we think they should. That should be a sure reminder that maybe that's not where God has placed us or wants us to go. So, how can we know? Let's look at some things to see if we can discover our purpose.

Beauty for Ashes (pg. 83)

For all the years you have suffered, God wants you to know He loves you so much and wants to turn your ashes into something beautiful. He wants to give you beauty for your ashes.

Read Isaiah 61:1-3. What are some things that the Lord has anointed us to do? Write them below.

_____
_____
_____
_____
_____
_____

Look at all those promises, lovelies. They are not only beautiful but they promise such great things. You are meant for so much more than what you've been allowed to believe of yourself, either by others or yourself.

God never meant for us to live in the pit of despair, depression, or any other dysfunction or disease. He meant to prosper us (Jeremiah 29:11). To live any other way is disobedience to Him, especially if you have been healed. So how do we turn things around?

Look at 2 Chronicles 7:14 (NKJV).

"If My people who are called by My name will humble themselves, and pray and seek My face, and turn from their wicked ways, then I will hear from heaven, and will forgive their sin and heal their land."

What is the first thing we must do? _____

When we become humble, we are taking our eyes off ourselves and placing them where they should have been all along: on God.

When we pray, seek God and turn from our disobedience, what does God promise to do? _____

There are people in the world, in our communities, who are suffering needlessly because someone somewhere told them God was punishing them. Those are not God's plans for you at all. God is not mad at you, lovely one. He has great big plans for all of us if we will only follow Him and look to Him for our guidance.

Water on the Rocks (pg. 87)

Like water running over the rocks in a mountain stream, smoothing the jagged edges over time, that's how God's Living Water runs over us. We have jagged edges in our lives caused by the things we have endured in the past. But when we follow God's plan for us, He begins to smooth the rough edges and mold us into who He created us to be.

Let's read Isaiah 43:18-19 from the Expanded Bible (EXB) and see what God says about our past.

"The LORD says, "Forget what happened before, and do not think about [consider; dwell on] the past. Look at the new thing I am going to do. It is already happening [sprouting/springing up]. Don't you see it? I will make a road [path; way] in the desert [wilderness; the return from Babylon is portrayed as a new Exodus] and rivers [streams] in the dry land [desert; wasteland].

When I read this version my heart sang!

What does it say the Lord says about what has happened in our past? _____
_____

What does He promise that He is going to do? _____
_____

God doesn't even want us to consider what happened before, in our past. Why? Because it's gone, it's done, *finite*. He wants us to look at what He's doing now. He has already started it. He wants us to see it. Do you see what He's doing in your life now?

Think about it for a minute, then write what you see God doing in your life now, on the lines below.

_____
_____
_____
_____
_____
_____

Now look at it and praise Him for giving you a purpose.

The things of our past can leave us feeling as if we are in the desert without a road or path to follow to get us out. In the desert, we could die of thirst. But when the streams of Living Water (Jesus) flow over and through us, He creates a new path for us. In addition, the river of new life that flows will smooth the rough edges like water on the rocks in the mountains. It quenches the thirst left by the desert of our past and causes new things in our life to spring forth. A new purpose from the healing, forgiveness, grace and hope that has come into us.

Overcoming Fear (pg. 89)

When God heals us and we step out into our new way of life, we often discover a newfound fear. Sometimes, the enemy will try to raise old fears to prevent us from walking out our purpose. God doesn't want us to be afraid, lovelies. That fear that's trying to creep back in is not from Him.

Read 2 Timothy 1:7 (NKJV) below.

"For God has not given us a spirit of fear, but of power and of love and of a sound mind."

What does it say that God has given us? _____

Fear does not come from God. It comes from our enemy, the devil. Those issues you gave to the Lord and He healed you from are gone. You don't have to pick them back up and allow them to cause you fear anymore.

God will however, use those things from your past to give encouragement and hope to others who are suffering the same things you once did. I know this from personal experience.

Read Genesis 50:20 and Romans 8:28.

What do the two have in common about how God works in our situations?
_____
_____

How many of our situations does God work for good? _____

God can take every situation we endure and use it for good. Every single one of them. He never leaves anything undone. With every issue buried deep within you, He can help you find your calling and healing. He will take every persecution and pain and put you on a course to victory and helping others.

Read Romans 8:37. What does it say that we are? _____
How do we become more than a conqueror? _____

No One Like You (pg. 95)

You are one unique lovely one. There is no one like you. Many times we grow up being compared to others in such a way that it gives us a complex and causes us to have low self-esteem or very little self-worth. But God made each of us different from the other. And He did it for a reason.

Look at Romans 12:4, 6(a) from the NKJV below.

"For as we have many members in one body, but all the members do not have the same function...Having then gifts differing according to the grace that is given to us, let us use them..."

We all have different spiritual gifts. We all have different talents. But we are all from the same spiritual family; God's family. Just like each of your body parts function in a different way, yet all from the same body, this is how it is in the Kingdom of God.

Look at the verse above again. Underline what it says about the function of the members.
What does it say about our gifts? _____

God wants us to use our gifts. He gave them to us to use. This is our purpose. God has a plan for you and has instilled in you something special. Don't compare yourself to others because you differ from them. Use your uniqueness to help someone else.

Don't Miss the Point (pg. 99)

God actually does have a purpose for you. You may still be wondering what that is. Don't miss the point. Jesus can, will, and wants to heal you. He has a purpose for you. But are you willing to step out in faith and walk in your purpose?

Many people go through life without ever knowing what their purpose is. Yet in truth, it's right under their noses the entire time. They miss the point because they refuse to see and refuse to step out in faith and get physical with walking out their purpose. We must realize that our purpose is not about us at all. It's all about Jesus. Even the Pharisees missed it because they were too focused on religious law and trying to intimidate anyone who professed Jesus.

Compare Isaiah 40:3 and John 1:23 then answer the questions below.
What was John the Baptist's purpose? _____
What is your purpose? _____

Now read John 1:26-27(NKJV) below.

"I baptize with water, but there stands One among you whom you do not know. It is He who, coming after me, is preferred before me, whose sandal strap I am not worthy to loose."

What was John declaring in this passage? _____
_____

John the Baptist's purpose was to lead the way to Jesus; to announce His arrival. In essence, John the Baptist was telling others about Jesus so they would follow Him. Your purpose and my purpose is the same thing; tell others about Jesus so that they will follow Him.

How we do that varies. We don't all have the same talents and gifts. What we do have will differ from one to another. But each one of us has something unique that will stand out to the people we are supposed to minister and witness to.

My purpose is to tell others how God healed me from depression, anxiety, intimidation, and mental and emotional abuse. The people I tell will either be people who are dealing with those things or they will be someone who knows someone who is suffering from them. When I'm prompted by the Holy Spirit to tell my story, I never know which end that person is on. Only after I've been obedient do I find out. Sometimes I find out immediately, other times it's later. But I must always be ready regardless. I don't choose the people I tell my story to, the Holy Spirit does. It's the same with you.

However God intends to use you, don't miss the point. Always be ready.

Answer the Phone (pg. 140)

You are chosen. You are anointed. You are gifted. You have what it takes. You have been appointed. You are on purpose. You were no accident. All the things you have gone through in your life were for a reason. You have a calling on your life. You have a purpose. Still looking to discover what that is?

Read Jeremiah 1:5-12 (I used NLT).

When does it say that God knew you? _____

What did He do? _____

In verse 7, where does the Lord say to go and what does He tell us to say? _____
_____

You may be thinking, no, He did that for Jeremiah. Okay. Let's look at some other verses.

Read 1 Corinthians 12:7, 18 (NLT) below.

"A spiritual gift is given to each of us so we can help each other... But our bodies have many parts, and God has put each part just where he wants it."

Just as He told Jeremiah to "go where I tell you to go" and "say what I tell you to say," He does the same with us today. Look again at the above verses. We each have a spiritual gift given to us by our heavenly Father. And just as God put each part where He wants it, so He has put each of us where He wants us.

Look again into 1 Corinthians 12:4-11 then list some of the spiritual gifts in the space below.

_____
_____
_____
_____

Who distributes all these gifts? _____
What does He decide? _____

You have a very special gift. God wants you to use it to help people. Your spiritual phone is ringing. Maybe it's time to answer it.

Leave Your Light On (pg. 148)

"The lights are on, but nobody's home!" We all deal with persecution. It's no different when we are walking healed. We are just equipped to handle it differently. As we talked about spiritual gifts on the last couple of pages, we need to know that as we use our gifts we shine a light for others to see. The outside world often tries to put out our light, whether physically, mentally, emotionally, or spiritually.

Read Matthew 5:14, 16(b). Write it below.

_____
_____
_____
_____

What does Jesus say we are to do? _____

Why are we to do this? _____

When we shine our light into a darkened world, people take notice. We draw two kinds of attention: positive and negative. We draw those who are seeking relief from the oppression and distress of their persecution and we draw those who want to intimidate us back into silence, thereby turning off our light. How do we discern the two?

In the first section of this study we read about putting on all of God's armor. I think as we get close to the end our study it would be good to revisit that passage, but I have a few more questions for you to answer and ponder.

Read Ephesians 6:10-17 then answer the questions below.

Why do we put on all of God's armor? _____
_____

Who are we fighting against? _____

If we put on all of God's armor, resist the enemy, what happens after the battle? ____
_____

We often forget a couple more things after we put on God's armor. It may very well be the most important weapon we can use.

Look at the passage below.

"Pray in the Spirit at all times and on every occasion. Stay alert and be persistent in your prayers for all believers everywhere. And pray for me, too. Ask God to give me the right words so I can boldly explain God's mysterious plan that the Good News is for Jews and Gentiles alike." ~Ephesians 6:18-19 (NLT)

How are we to pray? _____
When are we to pray? _____
What are we to ask God to give us? _____
_____
How are we to explain the Good News (tell others about God's plan)? _____

When we forget to pray, especially in the Spirit, we are neglecting to engage God and allow His Holy Spirit to guide us as we walk healed and into the purpose God has called us for.

We are called to be bold in our walk with God, not passive. Our light should always be on, but we also don't always have to answer the door, especially when the enemy comes looking for a fight. Instead, we can let faith answer the door and the enemy will run.

Reckless (pg. 184)

When we serve God, many times the obvious is overlooked. God often puts things and people out there for us yet sometimes we are so caught up in our everyday lives that we miss the obvious. We need to be reckless. We need to jump in with both feet and run with whatever it is that He has given us to do.

There is no reason to be afraid. We can be confident that if God has called us to do something, He will be right there with us to see it through.

Take a look at Romans 8:31 below from the NLT.

"What shall we say about such wonderful things as these? If God is for us, who can ever be against us?"

To be called to do something for God is not only humbling but exciting. If He calls you no one can be against you, though some will try.

Read Jeremiah 29:11. Write the plans God has for you below.

_____
_____

If God's plans for us are good and to give us a future and a hope, what more do we need? There is no way anyone can stop you from carrying out your purpose. Once you figure that out and know He has told you to move forward, you should be giddy with excitement.

If you look on page 186 of *Walking Healed* you'll see that I wear mismatched socks and have purple hair. Actually, it may say that I used to have purple hair. But at this writing, the hair is back to purple. Why? It's my ministry. I get attention from people who see the hair. It's a segue to be able to tell them about what God has done for me. It's reckless. I am a fifty-year-old grandmother who loves life and especially the new life He gave me when He healed me.

You don't have to have purple hair or wear mismatched socks to be reckless for God. He has given you a unique calling that only you can fulfill. Think about it.

On the lines below, write some ideas that just popped into your head:

_____
_____
_____
_____
_____

What are you interested in? What is your passion? What creeps into your thoughts many times a day when you're doing mundane things that don't require thinking? Could that be God planting your purpose inside your heart? How can you know?

Ask Him. Go to Him seriously, humbly, and without doubt or fear. Seek Him. Then do what He tells you. Ask for discernment. Ask for wisdom to know. You don't need a billboard with a bright neon flashing light. Just get quiet, hand everything over to Him and then listen.

Oh dear lovelies, your purpose is right there waiting for you. Maybe a godly friend has already given you the message from the Lord. What are you doing with it? Step out in faith today and walk healed. Walk in forgiveness, grace, hope, and in your purpose. When you do, you will meet others along the way that you can help, too. That's part of the plan, part of the purpose. While you're at it, tell them about Jesus.

Snakes in the Garden (pg. 203)

We can't end this section without a warning. Once you find your purpose, watch out for snakes. Have you ever walked out into your garden, or your yard, and come upon a snake? Maybe you aren't afraid of snakes. I wouldn't go as far as to say I'm afraid of them, I just don't like them. To come upon one certainly is a surprise.

It's the same with walking healed. Once you are healed, you begin to walk in your healing. Then forgiveness. Then you begin to show grace. Then you walk in hope. Eventually, if you haven't discovered it already, you find your purpose. That's when the snakes really come out. It's not that they aren't there to begin with. They are. But snakes lie in wait for you to drop your guard, become distracted, or get comfortable in your walk before they slither up and cause more issues.

When God created the universe and everything in it, He saw that it was good (check out Genesis 1). But when God gave Adam and Eve explicit instructions about what they could and could not do, that's when the enemy slithered in (literally) and messed things up.

Read Genesis 3:1-7

What did the serpent (snake) ask the woman? _____

_____

After she answered him, what did he tell her then? _____

The serpent blatantly lied to Eve about what God had said. He twisted God's words trying to trick Eve into doing what God said not to do.

What happened after the serpent said all these things to her? _____
_____

Isn't it just like an enemy? To disguise himself as something else in order to trick you into thinking or acting or even speaking a certain way to get you to mess up? Once you've done that, he then begins to ridicule or condemn you, again trying to trick you into believing you've gone too far and God can't use you anymore. Or he tries to convince you that you've completely messed up your healing or your walk or ministry. That simply is not true, dear ones. It's another lie of the enemy, the father of lies, to prevent you from living abundantly as God planned. Let's go back over a verse we've already covered just as a review.

Read 1 John 1:9 (NLT) below:

"But if we confess our sins to him, he if faithful and just to forgive us our sins and to cleanse us from all wickedness."
Once we confess (admit) our sins to him, what does it say he does? _____
_____

The New King James Version says He cleanses us from all unrighteousness. Face it, if we are being disobedient to God, it's bad, it's wicked, unrighteous, evil—all of those things. But the above verse says if we confess it to Jesus He will forgive us and cleanse us from all of it.

Not only will the enemy try to trick you, he will also use others to cause you trip up. He will even use the people closest to you to do it. The important thing is to remember that when God changes your life, nothing is the same. You begin a new journey. Any time you set out to serve God you will come across snakes in your garden. Don't let them deceive you, lovely ones. Make up your mind now and tell him no. Get the snakes out of your garden and keep them out.

A Time of Prayer

You have hopefully found your purpose or at least come close. On the lines provided below, write a prayer asking God to reveal your purpose to you and to help you walk in it. Choose a Scripture from the lessons or a memory verse to use to help you walk out your purpose.

_____
_____
_____
_____
_____
_____
_____
_____
_____
_____
_____
_____
_____
_____
_____
_____
_____
_____
_____
_____
_____

BEFORE WE SAY GOOD-BYE

We've come to the end of our journey together. I truly hope that through the pages of *Walking Healed* and this companion study that you have found healing, forgiveness for others and for yourself. I hope you have been able to extend grace and begin to walk in the hope that God has for you. But also I truly hope you have discovered your purpose. It all goes together, sweet one. He truly does work everything together for good. Everything the Lord does, He does it for you. If you haven't come to that realization yet, you will soon.

Everything the Lord does, He does it for you.

Walking Healed is an everyday journey. We must choose every day to walk in all the things we studied in the last few weeks. Not all of it will come all at once. Only through perseverance and making a choice to live in healing, forgiveness, grace and hope, then walking in your purpose every day will you begin to see each one take shape in your everyday life. Little by little you will grow and your light will shine brighter and brighter.

Use this workbook as your personal journal as you walk healed each day. Whenever you come across something that stumps you, look back over the pages and refresh your memory. Read the memory verses each day. Add new ones to grow in spirit and in the knowledge of God's Word.

My prayer for you as we journey on our separate ways is that you continue to walk in a way that others will see Jesus in you, see the change in you, and desire that difference in you. Show them Jesus, dear ones. Introduce them to Him. After all, that's part of your purpose.

If we never meet in person here, I'll see you over there someday.

Love,

Shelley

APPENDIX A: HOW TO MEMORIZE SCRIPTURE

As I was writing this study my Round Table Group asked me how I knew where to look for the Scriptures found in each lesson. I was asked, "How can I learn to do that?"

It made me start to wonder, with the contents of the book and the companion study, wouldn't a couple memory verses in each section help us on our journey?

If you're anything like I was, just the phrase "memory verse" causes a little anxiety. But memorizing God's Word is like nourishing our soul. In truth, that's exactly what it is. It's food for our soul. If we don't memorize God's Word, putting it in our hearts, we begin to starve spiritually.

Psalm 119:11 states, "Your word I have hidden in my heart that I may not sin against You." (NKJV) In the same chapter, verse 105 states, "Your word is a lamp to my feet And a light to my path."

Without God's Word in our hearts, how can it light the way on our journey? How can we know which way to turn? How can we be encouraged along the way? Also, how can we encourage others on their journey? This section covers how to put God's Word in our hearts so that as we journey we can do it with confidence and boldness.

Many people are intimidated at the mere thought of Scripture memory. Don't let it daunt you. It's really not hard. In fact, it's not only good for your soul, it's good for your brain.

I once taught a Christ-centered health program that required reciting a memory verse each week as part of several commitments. This gave many people great anxiety. But it shouldn't have. Memorizing Scripture is not a contest to see who can win. If you memorize even one, you win! Everyone wins. So relax.

The most elementary form of memorization, I think, is to write out the verse ten (10) times on a piece of paper or in a notebook. Index cards even work really well. Don't just write it, but also write the name of the book, chapter and verse. Include the translation you used, for example, NLT, NKJV, KJV, AMP, NIV, etc. Use a variety of translations so you can learn different perspectives. Make yourself a memory verse notebook and refer to it often.

Another way to memorize is to use an audio version and let it be read to you. That may be a bit more difficult but sometimes hearing it causes us to remember. Besides, it also increases our faith.

"So then faith comes by hearing, and hearing by the word of God."
~Romans 10:17 (NKJV)

Another way to memorize is by reading it out loud to yourself. Repeatedly. What this also accomplishes is when you read God's Word back to Him, you engage Him in conversation. He loves that.

He will begin to do wonderful things in and around you.

As you hide God's word in your heart He will begin to do wonderful things in and around you. You will be amazed and also delighted at all the awesome things He shows you. But more than that, you will be able to recall in an instant any verse that you need at the time you need it.

Knowing God's Word by memory will help you in every step of your journey to healing, forgiveness, grace, hope, and finding your purpose. It is my prayer that you gain much more than that in your journey walking healed.

WALKING HEALED MEMORY VERSES

The memory verses were taken from the study. They are in many different translations. I personally like the New Living Translation (NLT). It's what I use most and is very easy to understand. Please feel free to look up different variations and memorize the ones that speak to you. There are two to three memory verses for each section. Try different ways to memorize and use the method that works best for you. But remember, the key is not in how you memorize, but that you do memorize. It's food for your soul and will help you grow spiritually.

Healing

"And do not be conformed to this world, but be transformed by the renewing of your mind, that you may prove what is that good and acceptable and perfect will of God." ~ Romans 12:2 (NKJV)

"O LORD, if you heal me, I will be truly healed; if you save me, I will be truly saved. My praises are for you alone!" ~Jeremiah 17:14 (NLT)

Forgiveness

"If you forgive those who sin against you, your heavenly Father will forgive you. But if you refuse to forgive others, your Father will not forgive your sins." ~ Matthew 6:14-15 (NLT)

"As far as the east is from the west, so far has He removed our transgressions from us." ~Psalm 103:12 (HSCB)

"If we confess our sins, He is faithful and just to forgive us our sins and to cleanse us from all unrighteousness." ~ 1 John 1:9 (NKJV)

Grace

"For the Lord God is a sun and shield; The Lord will give grace and glory; No good thing will He withhold from those who walk uprightly." ~ Psalm 84:11 (NKJV)

"And He said to me, "My grace is sufficient for you, for My strength is made perfect in weakness…" ~ 2 Corinthians 12:9(a) (NKJV)

Hope

"My defense and shield depend on God, Who saves the upright in heart." ~ Psalm 7:10 (Amplified Bible)

"And now, Lord, what do I wait for and expect? My hope and expectation are in You."
    ~ Psalm 39:7 (Amplified Bible)

Finding Your Purpose

"But forget all that – it is nothing compared to what I am going to do. For I am about to do something new. See, I have already begun! Do you not see it? I will make a pathway through the wilderness. I will create rivers in the dry wasteland." ~ Isaiah 43:18-19 (NLT)

"For God has not given us a spirit of fear, but of power and of love and of a sound mind."
    ~ 2 Timothy 1:7 (NKJV)

"What shall we say about such wonderful things as these? If God is for us, who can ever be against us?" ~ Romans 8:31 (NLT)

ENDNOTES

Section One: Healing

   Part One, Spiritual

   Jeremiah 17:14, NLT

   Romans 12:2, NKJV

   John 10:10, NKJV

   Breaking the Chains

   God Can Still Use You

   Take Off Your Mask

   Isaiah 54:17, NLT

   Shields Up!

   Healing Rain

   Psalm 25:1-7, NKJV

   Freedom

   Make Up Your Mind

   Got Junk in Your Trunk?

   2 Corinthians 10:3-6, NKJV

   Short Circuited

   Stop People Pleasing

   Luke 1:46-47, 49, Amplified Bible

   1 Thessalonians 4:1(a), NLT

   Healing Part Two, Physical

   James 5:14-15, NKJV

   Psalm 142:1-2, NLT

   Lamentations 3:36, NLT

Section Two: Forgiveness

   Part One, Forgiveness for Others

   Matthew 6:14-15, NLT

   Matthew 18:21-22, NKJV

   Luke 23:34, KJV

   Mending Fences

   Romans 16:17-18, NKJV

   1 Peter 5:8-9, HCSB

   Offense and Defense

   Galatians 5:1, HCSB

   James 4:7-8, NLT

   Ephesians 6:13, NKJV

   Get Rid of Your "BUT!"

   John 21:20-22, NKJV

   Past is Past

   Psalm 103:12, HCSB

   Setting Boundaries

   Wisdom in Reconciling

   James 3:17, HCSB

   James 1:5-6(a), NKJV

   When Friendships Fail

   Ephesians 4:32, NLT

   Learning to Let God

   Zombies…the Walking Wounded

   Psalm 34:15, 17, NLT

   Psalm 118:17, Amplified Bible

   Psalm 147:3, Amplified Bible

   Unlocking Your Door

   2 Corinthians 12:9(a), NKJV

Forgiveness Part Two, Forgiving Yourself
   Do Yourself a Favor
   1 John 1:9, NKJV
   Colossians 3:13, NLT
   Jeremiah 33:3, NKJV

Section Three: Grace
   Psalm 84:11, NKJV
   Extending Grace (Giving Grace to Others)
   Moving Forward
   Colossians 4:2, HCSB
   Colossians 4:5-6, NLT
   Grace Who?
   Dictionary.com definition of grace
   Psalm 84:11, NKJV
   James 4:6, NKJV
   Comfort Training
   2 Corinthians 1:4, NLT
   Acts 1:8(b), NIV
   James 1:2-3, NLT
   1 Peter 5:9, NKJV
   2 Corinthians 12:9(a), NKJV
   My Chains Are Gone
   John 8:36, Amplified Bible
   Proverbs 18:10, Amplified Bible
   Psalm 61:3, Amplified Bible
   Extending Grace
   Because I Love You
   Ephesians 2:10, NLT
   Ephesians 2:4-8, NLT

   Don't Back Up
   Philippians 3:12, NLT
   Philippians 3:13(a), NLT
   What Are You Doing Here?
   1 Kings 19:3(a), 9, NLT
   Psalm 139:1, 7, NLT
   Where Do I Go From Here?
   Romans 16:17, NKJV
   Matthew 6::15, NKJV

Section Four: Hope
   Psalm 39:7, Amplified Bible
   Definition of hope, Siri, Apple iPhone
   Jeremiah 29:11-13, NLT
   Perfectly, Powerfully, Permanently
   Galatians 5:22-23, NLT
   Moving On
   John 14:6, NLT
   Can't Keep Me Down
   Psalm 7:10, Amplified Bible
   Psalm 39:7, Amplified Bible
   Where Do I Fit In?
   Ephesians 2:10, NLT
   Ch-Ch-Ch-Changes
   Philippians 3:21, NLT
   Lamentations 3:22-23, ESV
   Philippians 4:19, NLT
   I Am a Lazarus
   John 11:14, HCSB
   Rose-Colored Glasses
   Ephesians 6:14, NLT

God's Favor…is NOW!

Romans 5:5, NLT

Far Out!

Discovering My More

Jeremiah 32:27, NKJV

Changing Your Life

Psalm 57:2-3, NLT

One More Thing

Hebrews 6:17-18, NIV

Numbers 23:19, NIV

Psalm 145:13, NIV

Section Five: Finding Your Purpose

Isaiah 43:18-19, NLT

Beauty for Ashes

2 Chronicles 7:14, NKJV

Water on the Rocks

Isaiah 43:18-19, EXB

Overcoming Fear

2 Timothy 1:7, NKJV

No One Like You

Romans 12:4, 6(a), NKJV

Don't Miss the Point

John 1:26-27, NKJV

Answer the Phone

1 Corinthians 12:7, 18, NLT

Leave Your Light On

Ephesians 6:18-19, NLT

Reckless

Romans 8:31, NLT

Snakes in the Garden

1 John 1:9, NLT

THE MISMATCHED SOCKS THEORY

Whenever people discover that I wear socks that don't match they have one of a couple of responses. They either point and giggle, or they begin to tell me how their daughter or granddaughter wears mismatched socks and how that's the *in* thing with teenagers now. But I'm not a teenager. I am a fifty-year-old grandmother who has no teenager in my household. Though I raised two daughters who never wore anything mismatched (and one son, we can't forget him) each of my kids gave me a grandson. My house is filled with boys.

So what is, by society's standards, a middle-aged grandmother doing wearing brightly colored mismatched socks?

The Mismatched Socks Theory began as a funny entry on a blog post whereby I told a little bit about myself. I wanted to make some of the entries funny so people would know that I like to laugh, can be funny, and that not everything I do is serious. Basically, I like to have fun. So I wrote that I like to wear mismatched socks. However, after that post I began to feel convicted because at the time I did not actually wear them. I only liked to do that for fun once in a while.

The Holy Spirit convicted me that day. After my healing, I was looking for unique ways to start a conversation with people without scaring them half to death with my excitement over what the Lord has done in my life. I was truly alive for the first time in my life and I wanted to tell others and help those who deal with the same things God healed me of. But how do I do that? That's when the Holy Spirit gave me the idea to actually wear mismatched socks and use them as a conversation piece.

Most people have a mismatched socks basket in their home. Those lonely socks that have lost their mate, so they get thrown into a basket with the hopes of finding said mate in the future. Yet, most of the time they get thrown out because the mate is never found. Well, I stopped doing that. You see, the socks don't match but they're still useful. They still have a purpose.

By wearing mismatched socks I discovered that I too, am a mismatched sock. I don't match anyone else. I don't fit in anywhere else. But God still loves me. He can still use me. And just like that lonely, mismatched sock, He plucked me out of the laundry basket of life, cleaned me up, and put me to use.

One by one I find other mismatched socks (people who are hurting) and I encourage them that they don't have to match anyone else or anything else. I encourage them that God has a purpose for them. He made them unique on purpose for a specific purpose. Though they wonder where they fit in, though they may believe that they don't fit in anywhere, I love to encourage them that they actually do fit in, and always have with God's great big plans for them.

We are *all* mismatched socks. There are no two who are alike. Even identical twins are different from one another. We are all unique, different, created by a loving, wonderful God who wants to do great things with each of us. I'll continue wearing mismatched socks. I'll also continue encouraging others. And if the socks help one person realize who they are in Christ, well then it was all worth it.

> *We are all unique, different, created by a loving, wonderful God who wants to do great things with each of us.*

ABOUT THE AUTHOR

Shelley Wilburn was born and raised in West Frankfort, Illinois. She began writing when she was twelve years old. She has written several articles and devotions for various newspapers, women's magazines, and newsletters. In addition to writing, Shelley is also an avid reader, book reviewer, blogger, and speaker. Using her love of writing, motorcycle riding, and wearing mismatched socks, Shelley has developed a unique ministry of encouraging others using biblical truths and stories from her own personal life. Shelley is married to her high school sweetheart D.A. and together they have celebrated over thirty years of marriage. They have three grown, married children and three grandsons.

Shelley loves to hear from her readers.
You can find Shelley at:

Her website: www.shelleywilburn.org
Facebook: www.facebook.com/authorshelleywilburn
Twitter: @Shelley_Wilburn
Pinterest: www.pinterest.com/shelleyawilburn
Instagram: www.instagram.com/shelleywilburn
E-mail her at shelley@shelleywilburn.org

A WORD ABOUT
Walking Healed, the Book

Written in diary form, Shelley Wilburn's book, *Walking Healed*, is her journey after being healed of over forty years of mental and emotional issues including depression, anxiety, and intimidation. Using snippets of her healing journey along with biblical truths, Shelley takes the reader on a journey of healing, forgiveness, grace and hope then leads into finding your purpose.

Written for those who suffer the pain and loneliness of depression and intimidation, Shelley reaches down into the black hole, finds those who are hurting and helps them find their way out.

Walking Healed will help the reader realize that even Christians suffer depression. Shelley Wilburn knows and understands this from her personal experience with depression and intimidation. She also knows the freedom from these issues when God heals you and takes you on a wonderful journey of walking healed. Shelley's story of healing helps others know that even depression is curable and "nothing is impossible with God."